W9-AOC-525

Supplement to

A Guide to Source Materials

for the Study of Barbados History

1627-1834

The John Carter Brown Library

gratefully acknowledges the assistance

of the following donors who helped

to make the publication of this work possible:

Mrs. Michael J. Chandler

Mrs. G. B. Tweedy

Mr. Joseph W. Ress

The Barbados Museum and Historical Society

"*Supplement to* A Guide to Source Materials for the Study of Barbados History, 1627-1834 "

By Jerome S. Handler

Published by
The John Carter Brown Library
and
The Barbados Museum and Historical Society

Providence, Rhode Island, 1991

The John Carter Brown Library is an independently funded and administered center for advanced research in the humanities at Brown University. For further information write to the Library at Box 1894, Providence, RI, 02912.

ISBN 0-916617-35-1

To the Memory

of

Michael J. Chandler, 1921-1984

Dear Friend and Valued Colleague

First Archivist of Barbados, 1964-1976

CONTENTS

ILLUSTRATIONS

The frontispiece and figure 1 are reproduced by permission of
the British Library. Figures 2, 3, 4 are published courtesy of the
Muséum d'Histoire Naturelle, Le Havre.

FOREWORD

The past is the mother of the present, but one of the great dangers lurking in that truth is the false belief that the order of things observed in the present is a trustworthy key to the past. The island of Barbados today does not play a great role in world affairs, but in the late 1600s most English statesmen considered it a far more important place than the undeveloped colonies on the North American mainland. Barbados, as a major plantation-slave society, was extremely productive of wealth and had the advantage also of being strategically located vis-a-vis the French and the Spanish. At the time, those were the considerations that really mattered.

From the moment of the first European colonization of the Western Hemisphere, initiated by Columbus, to the early nineteenth century, the West Indies (or the Caribbean) played an enormously important role in the history of the Americas. For a true picture of the Western Hemisphere in those 300 years, looked at from almost any perspective, it is usually essential to take into account the state of affairs in the Caribbean, with Barbados being among the very most significant of the islands. Such a point of view is not one that we are used to.

It is for the above reasons that the John Carter Brown Library for one hundred years or more has been collecting material relative to the islands—in Spanish, French, Dutch, English, Danish, Swedish, etc.—and why the bibliographic work that Professor Jerome Handler has been engaged in concerning Barbados for over two decades is so important. This substantial supplement to the original Handler *Guide* (published in 1971) will be of great use to all students of the past of the Americas and of English expansion to the New World. It will also be of critical help to the researchers who come to the JCB every year who wish to work with our Caribbean holdings. With Handler's *Guide* and, now, its *Supplement* in hand, they will be able to accomplish their research tasks with maximum efficiency.

This book could not have been published without outside financial support. It is a pleasure to acknowledge here the

xiii

generosity of Mrs. Joan Chandler, Mrs. Gordon Tweedy, and Mr. Joseph Ress, whose contributions have helped to make the publication of this work possible. We are also grateful to the Barbados Museum and Historical Society for its willingness to be a co-publisher and sponsor of the project, in particular the president of the BMHS, Dr. Trevor A. Carmichael, and the director of the museum, Ms. Alissandra Cummins. I wish to thank, too, Professor Peter Roberts of the University of the West Indies who was of great help to the project at a critical moment.

Norman Fiering
Director and Librarian
John Carter Brown Library

PREFACE

The early history of Barbados is that of a quintessential New World slave society. Shortly after the island was colonized in 1627, it began to develop an export economy that at first mainly depended on the relatively small-scale cultivation of tobacco and cotton, largely produced by free and indentured whites. By the 1640s, however, sugar was being grown on a commercial scale, and the development of plantations as the major sugar production units was stimulated. With the sugar plantations came slave labor from Africa. Barbados was the first territory in England's overseas empire to develop large-scale sugar cane cultivation under a plantation system dependent on African slave labor. By the 1650s the island was already a developed plantation-slave society. Throughout the last half of the seventeenth century and into the early eighteenth, it was England's wealthiest and most populous colony in the Americas. During the 1670s Barbados reached the zenith of its prosperity, and its black population of about 32,800 far exceeded that of any other English territory; the number of blacks in Barbados was almost double the total in England's five other Caribbean colonies and close to six times the total of blacks in all of England's mainland colonies combined. It was in Barbados that black and white confronted each other earlier and on a larger scale than anywhere else in English America. Although Barbados's prominence in England's sugar empire was preempted by Jamaica during the third decade or so of the eighteenth century, the island continued to be dominated by the slave production of sugar under the plantation system.

In the mid-1960s, I began a research project that was designed to produce an intensive and holistic picture of the life of Barbados's slaves, particularly those who worked on plantations. This research was intended to recapture, in as much detail as possible, the physical condition of slaves and their social and cultural life, and to chart changes in their lives over time. To achieve maximum insight into developmental processes and sociocultural change, I intended the research to treat the entire slave period of some 200 years, from early colonization to 1834, the year slavery ended throughout the British Empire.

In 1971, as a by-product of this research, I published *A Guide to Source Materials for the Study of Barbados History, 1627-1834* (Carbondale: Southern Illinois University Press). In the course of trying to obtain information from historical sources, I worked in scores of libraries and archival repositories in the United States, Europe, and the West Indies. Most of the consulted items had little or no bearing on slave life, but many helped shed light on the early history of this important New World slave society. The *Guide* was published in order to bring these source materials to the attention of a wider scholarly audience. It describes or mentions Barbados-related manuscripts or manuscript collections in about sixty-five repositories, discusses and locates copies of early newspapers, describes Barbadian materials in the British *Parliamentary Papers*, and identifies approximately 654 different published titles which, in one form or another, constitute primary sources relating to Barbados's early history. With relatively few exceptions, printed materials are annotated and given at least one library location.

Since the *Guide*'s publication, my research on Barbados slavery has continued and has yielded many new printed items and manuscripts as well as information that clarifies some of the entries in the *Guide*; in addition, I have continued to develop bibliographic interests that are specifically directed to identifying source materials pertaining to the island's early history. The present *Supplement* represents the culmination of a number of years of additional research and includes approximately 270 printed items. About 92 percent of these were not included in the *Guide* ; others were included but not annotated, for reasons that are given where appropriate in the following pages.

With close to twenty-five years of research experience in the early history of the British West Indies and Barbados, I am reasonably confident that there no longer exist any nonidentified printed works of major consequence relating to the period covered by this *Supplement* and the *Guide* that preceded it. On the other hand, although this *Supplement* includes some previously unreported manuscripts and manuscript collections, undoubtedly there are others which may never be publicly identified or which will only come to light in future years. As Michael J. Chandler noted in a review of the 1971 *Guide*, "new manuscripts are always coming to light and every fresh comer to the field will be able to add to the tally of these" (*JBMHS*, 34, 1973,151).

I assume that users of this *Supplement* also will have access to the *Guide*. The preface to the latter describes the criteria and procedures employed in its compilation, but some of the major features can be repeated here since they are also followed in this *Supplement*.

Although some of the voluminous contemporary literature treating the West Indies in general also has bearing on Barbados history, in this *Supplement,* as in the *Guide*, I have generally tried to include published materials only if they mentioned Barbados in their titles or treated the island in their contents; also included, even if they do not meet these criteria, are titles published in Barbados and those authored by persons known to be Barbadian-born or long-term island residents. Some of the items included in this *Supplement* may appear to have little research value, but it is for the researcher himself to determine what is of value. Thus, as a guiding principle, I continue to follow H. I. Hogbin's observation on a bibliography of the Pacific: "Some of the minor publications, it may be thought, would have been decently left in oblivion. But . . . subsequent generations may well discover significant material in the most unlikely places" (quoted in L. Comitas, *Caribbeana 1900-1965* [Seattle, 1968], pp. *viii-ix*).

The vast majority of the sources listed here were published prior to 1834, that is during the slave period, but some later items have been included because they contain firsthand information which easily could be applicable to earlier years. In addition, some of these later items, including those published relatively recently, are included if they are transcriptions of manuscripts written during the slave period.

Many of the printed works relating to early Barbados history are found in very few libraries; not even the largest libraries, such as the Library of Congress or the British Library, contain all of them. In most cases I have identified at least one library where the item may be found. This library may be the one in which I consulted the item or it may be the one in which an authoritative source has given its location. I made no attempt to survey all of the holdings in each of the libraries visited. It is to be understood, then, that the library I have cited for a published item may not be the only one in which it is located. I usually made an effort to locate an item even if I had no opportunity to examine it personally. In other cases, which are commented on in the annotations, a widespread search failed to yield even a single extant copy. This was particularly the case for materials published in Barbados during the eighteenth century and the first several decades of the nineteenth; such items were consistently the most difficult to locate. All nonconsulted printed items are given a source for the citation and are identified with an asterisk (*) preceding the author/title entry; manuscripts not personally examined are clearly specified, and the sources for these manuscripts are given.

For each published entry I have given the author's name (if known), title, place and date of publication, and the number of volumes or pages. I have indicated the number of volumes or pages in printed items to give the user some idea of the physical scope of the work. I am fully aware, however, that this information is often crude and does not conform to the standards of the professional bibliographer. Items identified as broadsheets are single sheets printed on two sides; broadsides are printed on one side. Library locations appear in abbreviation in brackets [ ] at the end of each entry or within the annotation itself. Most of the abbreviations used in this *Supplement* are the same as those used in the original *Guide*, a notable exception being the British Library [BL] which was formerly referred to as the British Museum [BM]; there are also some new libraries that were not included in the *Guide*. If the author's name, or the date and place of publication, is not printed in the work itself, such information, if known, is given in brackets, and I have tried to indicate my reasons or sources for ascribing authorship or imprint data. The annotation of an item attempts to give, at the minimum, an indication of its major emphasis and the types of materials contained within it.

I have included some manuscripts and manuscript collections that were not mentioned in the *Guide*, but I have made no effort to update the manuscript holdings in the Barbados Department of Archives. These were described for the *Guide* by Michael J. Chandler. Researchers should be aware, however, that since the *Guide*'s publication, the Department of Archives has made some additions to its pre-1834 materials. Finally, a self-evident point to scholars may nonetheless merit emphasis. Many items relating to the British West Indies in general, such as tracts arguing the pros and cons of slavery and the slave trade or Britain's commercial interests in the Caribbean, often do not mention particular islands or they cite only a few of them; the issues discussed in such works can often be directly relevant to Barbados, but have not been included in the *Guide* or in this *Supplement*.

ACKNOWLEDGMENTS

Research for this *Supplement* has been going on for many years in a number of libraries and repositories, but the most intensive work took place during several summers in the 1980s, especially in 1985 and 1988 while I held fellowships at the John Carter Brown Library. I am greatly indebted to Norman Fiering, Director of the JCB, for his continuous encouragement and assistance, and to the JCB's professional and administrative staff, particularly Susan Danforth, Ilse Kramer, Susan Newbury, Elaine Shiner, and Karen DeMaria and Lynne Harrell; the high quality of their professionalism and the congenial personal ambience they provided did much to make research at the JCB such a pleasurable experience. I must also thank various staff members of the British Library. Although I never learned their names, their assistance on numerous occasions over the past twenty or so years contributed to the many rewards of being a reader at that impressive institution.

I am particularly grateful to Samuel J. Hough, the former Assistant Librarian at the JCB, with whom I initially collaborated in compiling addenda to my 1971 *Guide*, and who was instrumental in helping me start the additional bibliographic work which has led to the present publication. The JCB's celebrated chronological index was an invaluable tool for identifying new materials and for developing bibliographic leads, and a number of items in this *Supplement* were also identified through some of the early volumes of *European Americana* . This important bibliographic project, which chronologically lists all publications relating to the Americas published in Europe from 1493 to 1750, is being carried out under the auspices of the JCB. (As of this writing, volumes 1 [1493-1600], 2 [1601-50], 5 [1701-25], and 6 [1726-50] have been published [New York: Readex Books, 1980, 1982, 1987, 1989], and volumes 3 and 4 [1651-1700] should be published in 1990.) The editor, Dennis Landis, immeasurably helped my research by permitting me to consult the detailed typescript indexes and entries for volumes 5 and 6 before they went into print; Landis has also been extremely helpful with other bibliographic queries and translation matters.

For assistance on various bibliographic issues, I also owe thanks to Peter Campbell, Philip Dark, Bridget Ikin, Paul Kelly, Richard Newman, Robin Price, Patricia M. Spacks, E. C. Wilkie, and Margaret Winters. Beatrice Moore graciously agreed to edit the manuscript. John McCusker, during a conversation at the JCB in July 1975, first suggested the idea of compiling this *Supplement,* and for many years Jack P. Greene has continuously encouraged this project. Final completion of the *Supplement* took place during 1989-90, while I was an Associate at the W.E.B. DuBois Institute for Afro-American Research at Harvard University.

ABBREVIATIONS

AAS   American Antiquarian Society (Worcester, Mass.)

BAN   Bancroft Library (University of California, Berkeley)

BL   British Library (London)

BMHS   Barbados Museum and Historical Society (St. Ann's Garrison, St. Michael)

BOA   Boston Athenaeum (Boston, Mass.)

CL   Clements Library (University of Michigan, Ann Arbor)

CU   Cambridge University Library (Cambridge, Eng.)

DNB   *Dictionary of National Biography*

EA   *European Americana*

ESTC   *Eighteenth-Century Short Title Catalog*

GIL   John Gilmore, "Bishop Coleridge: A Bibliography of His Printed Works," *JBMHS* 36, 1979, 50-65

H   Harvard University (Cambridge, Mass.)

HL   Huntington Library (San Marino, Calif.)

JBMHS   *Journal of the Barbados Museum and Historical Society* (Bridgetown, Barbados)

JCB   The John Carter Brown Library (Providence, R.I.)

JSH-71   Jerome S. Handler, *A Guide to Source Materials for the Study of Barbados History, 1627-1834* (Carbondale, Ill., 1971)

KEI   Kenneth E. Ingram, *Manuscripts Relating to Commonwealth Caribbean Countries in United States and Canadian Repositories* (Barbados, 1975)

LC   Library of Congress (Washington, D.C.}

LCP   The Library Company of Philadelphia (Philadelphia, Pa.)

LJR   L. J. Ragatz, *A Guide for the Study of British Caribbean History, 1763-1834* (Washington, D. C., 1932)

NL   Newberry Library (Chicago, Ill.)

NSTC   *Nineteenth-Century Short Title Catalog*

NUC   *National Union Catalog* (Washington, D. C.)

NYHS   New-York Historical Society (New York, N.Y.)

NYPL   New York Public Library (New York, N.Y.)

O-BO   Oxford University, Bodleian Library (Oxford, Eng.)

O-TR   Oxford University, Trinity College (Oxford, Eng.)

PRO   Public Record Office (London)

PW   Peter Walne, ed., *A Guide to Manuscript Sources for the History of Latin America and the Caribbean in the British Isles* (London, 1973)

| RS | Robert Schomburgk, *History of Barbados* (London, 1848) | URB | University of Illinois Library (Urbana) |
| SIU | Southern Illinois University Library (Carbondale) | UWI | University of the West Indies (Mona, Jamaica) |

Supplement to

A Guide to Source Materials

for the Study of Barbados History

1627-1834

Printed Books, Pamphlets, Broadsheets, Broadsides, Maps

1645-1750

COPPIER, GUILLAUME
Histoire et voyage des Indes Occidentales, et de plusiers autres regions maritimes et esloignées.
Lyons, 1645. *206 pp.*   [NYPL, JCB, LC]
A few comments on Barbados (p. 25), "la premiere des isles de l'Amerique," and its economy, but the author's ship only passed the island and did not stop.

BULLOCK, WILLIAM
Virginia impartially examined.
London, 1649. *66 pp.*   [JCB]
Designed to encourage settlers to Virginia where they might "raise their fortunes," a paragraph on Barbados (pp. 31-32) lauds the island's wealth and economic vitality and offers some reasons for same.

HUNT, ROBERT
The Island of Assada, neere Madagascar impartially defined.
[London, 1650]. *8 pp.*   [BL]
Writing this tract to encourage settlers, Hunt, the governor of Assada (which he locates at about nine miles from Madagascar) describes the island's geography and its agricultural and commercial potential; brief comparisons are occasionally made with Barbados, but virtually nothing is said about Barbados per se. The publication date is inscribed in a contemporary hand on the title page.

A PERFECT diurnall of some passages and proceedings of, and in relation to the armies in England and Ireland: licensed according to the direction of the late act for printing.
London [1650, 1652].   [NL]
Included in the NL's Ayer collection, this newsletter with consecutive pagination

seems to have appeared weekly. It reports on the English Civil War from a parliamentarian perspective. The NL has numbers 31 (July 8-15, 1650), containing two brief paragraphs relating to the Cavalier-Roundhead struggle for Barbados (pp. 359-60), 34 (July 29-August 5, 1650), with similar, albeit briefer, news (pp. 402-3), 108 (December 29, 1651-January 5, 1652), containing a somewhat lengthier account on the same theme as well as a copy of a Barbados act of September 12, 1651 "for the sequestration of delinquent estates" (pp. 1560-63).

H., T.
A true and exact narrative of the proceedings of the parliaments fleet, against the island of Barbados . . . .
London, 1652. *12 pp.*   [JCB]
Written by a pro-parliamentarian "eye witness" while in Carlisle Bay, this item deals with George Ayscue's taking of Barbados from the royalists in 1651/52 and treats the political issues and military activities involved. The subtitle is "An exact narrative of the reducing of the island of Barbados, etc."

GORGES, FERDINANDO
America painted to the life . . . . With a perfect relation of our English discoveries . . . and plantations of our English in Virginia, New-England, and Berbadoes.
London, 1659. *57 pp.*   [JCB, BL]
Incomplete at the author's death, this was finished by his grandson (of the same name). It is the first part of a three-part work, each part of which was separately published. Despite the mention of

"Berbadoes" in the title, the island is only mentioned once (p. 4), where its colonization in 1627 is noted. Evidently the author had originally intended to deal at length with Barbados but death intervened.

[FOX, GEORGE]
An epistle . . . . to be sent abroad among the saints scattered in old and new England . . . Barbadoes, and Virginia.
London, 1660. *16 pp.*   [JCB]
A religious epistle, written from London and signed "G.F."

PINDER, RICHARD
A loving invitation (to repentance, and amendment of life) unto all the inhabitants of the island Barbados.
London, 1660. *16 pp.*   [BL]
Listed in JSH-71, but not consulted. Written during a visit to Barbados in 1660, this Quaker tract strenuously admonishes Barbadian whites, and bitingly condemns their behavior and a way of life that is "given to the lusts and pleasures of this evil world." In an unusual statement for the period, Pinder unequivocally urges masters to treat their slaves and indentured servants better and to avoid "cruell usage, for that the Lord hates [since] they are of the same blood and mould you are of."

BERKELEY, WILLIAM
A discourse and view of Virginia.
[London? 1663?]. *12 pp.*   [BL, HL]
In making a case for Virginia's importance to England and its potential for economic development, comparative comments are occasionally offered on the economic state of the West Indies in general and Barbados, "the mistresse of them all," in particular.

LONG, ANTHONY, HILTON, WILLIAM, AND FABIAN, PETER
A relation of a discovery lately made on the coast of Florida . . . by William Hilton . . . with Capt. Anthony Long and Peter Fabian in the ship Adventure, which set sayl from Spike's Bay Aug. 10, 1663. And was set forth by several gentlemen and merchants of the island of Barbadoes.
London, 1664. *34 pp.*   [JCB, H, BL]
Containing no information on Barbados per se, most of this work (pp. 1-22) details the experiences with Indians and Spaniards of a Barbadian party sent to explore the possibilities of colonizing

South Carolina. On January 6, 1664, the *Adventure* safely returned to Carlisle Bay. The "accompt of our discovery" is signed at the end by Anthony Long, William Hilton, and Peter Fabian, in that order, although library catalogs will sometimes list William Hilton as the author. Pages 23-28 contain a few letters between William Hilton and the Spanish governor at St. Helena, and pp. 29-34 are a copy of agreements made by Thomas Modyford and Peter Colleton of Barbados with persons who would settle South Carolina, including an award of 1,000 acres of land each to Long, Hilton, and Fabian. This item has been reprinted in Peter Force, ed., *Tracts and Other Papers* (Washington, D.C., 1846, vol. 4, no. 2) and in Alexander Salley, ed., *Narratives of Early Carolina, 1650-1708* (New York, 1911, pp. 37-61).

JOURNAEL, GEHOUDEN op's landts-schip de spiegel, van't gene gepasseert en verricht . . . Michiel de Ruyter.
Amsterdam, 1665. *82 pp.*   [JCB]
Includes a brief, apparently eyewitness, account of the 1665 attack on Barbados (pp. 65-66) by the Dutch admiral De Ruyter; the only time in the island's history that a large foreign force sailed into Bridgetown's harbor.

A BRIEF description of the province of Carolina on the coasts of Floreda.
London, 1666. *10 pp.*   [JCB]
Mentions (p. 4) the food crops brought to Carolina from Barbados.

COALE, JOSIAH
The books and divers epistles of the faithful servant of the Lord Josiah Coale.
London, 1671. *343 pp.*   [JCB]
Coale was one of a number of English Quakers who visited Barbados's Quaker community during the last half of the seventeenth century. Three of the epistles in this posthumously published volume were signed and dated at Barbados in 1661 (pp. 47-50, 90-95, 95-104), but none contain any information about the island.

JANEWAY, JAMES
Mr. James Janeway's legacy to his friends, containing twenty seven famous instances of Gods providences in and about sea dangers and deliverances.
London, 1674. *134 pp.*   [JCB]
Four of these accounts of "miraculous" escapes from dangers at sea relate to

Barbados. In 1668, a ship almost sank en route from New England to Barbados; another arrived at the island around 1664 after having narrowly escaped a mutiny during the voyage (pp. 34-37, 43). In the 1660s, a ship traveling from Barbados to Virginia transported an Irish woman, an indentured servant; punished for her recalcitrance, she threatened the ship with an unsafe passage. This brief account, relating the voyage's difficulties and the woman's rebellious behavior, offers an unusual example of the assertiveness and independence of a female indentured servant (pp. 44-47). Finally, West Africans captured and held for ransom some of the crew of an English slaver; ultimately freed, their ship safely arrived at Barbados in 1668 (pp. 73-87). Later editions (London, 1708, 1721 [BL]) contain the same accounts.

DUVAL, PIERRE
La geographie universelle.
Paris, 1676. *312 pp.*   [JCB]
Contains a conventional description of Barbados, geographical, historical, and commercial (pp. 57-58).

DASSIE, F.
Description generale des costes de l'Amerique.
Rouen, 1677. *421 pp.*   [JCB]
Includes a very brief paragraph (p. 123) describing Barbados's geography.

PIELAT, BARTHELEMY
La Vie . . . du Sr. Michel De Ruyter.
Rouen, 1678. *362 pp.*   [JCB]
Provides a brief, firsthand account of De Ruyter's 1665 attack on Barbados (p. 155).

BLOME, RICHARD
A geographical description of the world, taken from the works of the famous monsieur Sanson.
[London], 1680. *493 pp.*   [JCB]
Contains a brief description (pp. 459-60) of Barbados's flora, fauna, agricultural products, economy, climate, parishes, towns, fortifications, and population. The description is very similar, albeit briefer, to Blome's 1672 description of Barbados (JSH-71).

MORDEN, ROBERT
Geography rectified: or, a description of the world.
London, 1680. *418 pp.*   [JCB]
Short, conventional description of

Barbados's location, climate, agricultural products, parishes, towns, forts, and population (pp. 397-99) which seems to be mostly derived from Ligon (1657); includes a map emphasizing coastal details (see T. Campbell, *The Printed Maps of Barbados*, The Map Collectors' Circle [London, 1965], p.11).

CAREW, THOMAS
Hinc illae lacrymae; or, an epitome of the life and death of Sir William Courteen and Sir Paul Pyndar.
London, 1681. *24 pp.*   [JCB, BL]
References to Barbados's early political and naval history, an account of its settlement, and the Courteen-Carlisle controversy, with its legal ramifications (pp. 2, 21-23).

[PENN, WILLIAM]
Some account of the province of Pennsylvania in America.
London, 1681. *10 pp.*   [JCB]
Designed to encourage settlers to Pennsylvania, Barbados is briefly mentioned (p. 2) in arguing that the colonies hold economic opportunities.

A., T. [AMY, THOMAS]
Carolina; or description of the present state of that country.
London, 1682. *40 pp.*   [JCB]
The description of Carolina's geography, trade, population, etc., often makes comparisons with the West Indies, primarily implying Jamaica or Barbados (where the author had lived or visited). In addition, Barbados is specifically mentioned in brief comments on the island's tar imports, sponges found along the coast, the continuing arrival of new settlers, and its general imports from Carolina. In a description of the hummingbird, the author (whose name is suggested in the JCB catalog) notes that Barbadian Jews "curiously skin these little birds, filling them with fine sand, and perfuming their feathers" and then export them to Europe "as pretty delicacies for ladies, who hang them at their breasts and girdles" (pp. 23-24).

F., R.
The present state of Carolina with advice to the setlers [sic].
London, 1682. *36 pp.*   [HL, JCB]
Reports that "several families" have come from Barbados and that the "settlement of

Albermarle" exports "good beef and pork" to Barbados and other islands. Author's name suggested in the JCB catalog.

BRANDT, GEERAERT
Het Leven en Bedryf . . . Michiel de Ruiter.
Amsterdam, 1687. *1,063 pp.*   [BL, LC]
A biography of De Ruyter, the celebrated Dutch admiral whose fleet attacked Barbados in 1665 (pp. 363-64); the island is also mentioned with respect to naval events on 15 September 1667 (p. 607) .

MORE, NICHOLAS
A letter from Doctor More, with passages out of several letters from persons of good credit.
[London], 1687. *11 pp.*   [JCB, BL, HL]
Designed to show the health of Pennsylvania's economy and agriculture, occasional references to Barbados mention Pennsylvania's trade with the island.

*AN ACCOUNT of the late dreadful earthquake in the island of Mevis [sic], St. Christophers, etc. which happen'd in the beginning of April, of this present year 1690. In a letter to a friend in London.
London, 1690. *Broadsheet.*   [JCB]
After describing an earthquake in Nevis, it is simply noted: "we are also informed . . . that the Barbadoes also has had some trembling fits, but not so considerable." The JCB copy contains the date, in a contemporary hand, of 24 June 1690.

BURNYEAT, JOHN
The truth exalted in the writings of that eminent and faithful servant of Christ John Burnyeat.
London, 1691. *284 pp.*   [JCB]
JSH-71 discusses a nineteenth century reprint. The 1691 edition, however, also contains epistles written from Barbados in 1665 and 1670 (pp. 103-4, 107-9), the latter arguing that a major epidemic, "where of many died," resulted from divine judgment.

THE INTEREST of the nation, as it respects all the sugar-plantations abroad, and refining of sugars at home . . . humbly offered to the . . . House of Commons.
London, 1691. *11 pp.*   [JCB]
Relating the poor economic state of England's sugar refiners and their relationship to importers of colonial muscavado sugar, this tract argues against

the colonial manufacture of sugar. Barbados is mentioned several times and it is maintained that the island's manufacture of clayed sugar alone "is destructive" to English sugar refiners and England's best economic interests.

*PLUKENET, LEONARD
L. Plukeneti phytographia . . . almagestum botanicum.
London, 1691-1705. *7 pts.*   [BL]
R. A. Howard, "Early botanical records from the West Indies, particularly Barbados" (*Botanical Journal of the Linnean Society* 79, 1979, 65-96, Appendix 2) lists twenty-nine references to Barbados plants in the Plukenet work.

CHILD, JOSIAH
A discourse concerning plantations.
London, 1692. *40 pp.*   [JCB]
Barbados is occasionally referred to in this essay which emphasizes the importance of England's American colonies to the English economy, and argues against the view that establishing plantations harms the economy of England by depopulating it.

BOHUN, EDMUND
A geographical dictionary.
London, 1693. *440 pp.*   [JCB]
Contains a conventional one-paragraph description (p. 36) of Barbados history, agricultural products, economy, water supplies, and climate. First published in London in 1688.

A BRIEF, but most true relation of the late barbarous and bloody plot of the Negro's in the island of Barbados on Friday the 21 of October, 1692 . . . In a letter to a friend.
London, 1693. *Broadsheet.*   [NL]
One of several planned revolts during the last half of the seventeenth century, this one was accidentally discovered the night before it was to take place, when two of the conspirators were overheard discussing "their wicked design." The slaves had intended to "kill the governour and all the planters, and to destroy the government there established, and to set up a new governour and government of their own." Planned by creole slaves, between two and three hundred were ultimately arrested;

"many were hang'd, and a great many burn'd. And (for a terror to the others) there are now seven hanging in chains, alive, and so starving to death." The unidentified author arrived at Barbados the night before the events he describes took place. At the end of this item, the name of the publisher Edward Bohun (see *DNB*) is printed along with his authorization for publication and the date January 18, 1693. This item is very rare; the NL copy may be unique.

RELATION DE ce qui s'est passe dans les isles de l'Amerique, ou les victoires . . . sur les Anglois par les troupes du roy.
[Bordeaux, 1693]. *4 pp.*   [JCB]
Dated Martinique, 6 May 1693, a description of the damage caused by an English military force, which included Barbados militiamen, and the retaliation of the French and their ultimate victory; captured prisoners included an unnamed lieutenant from Barbados.

SALMON, WILLIAM
  Seplasium. The compleat English physician.
  London, 1693. *1,207 pp.*   [JCB]
This encyclopedic work gives the medicinal properties of hundreds of materials, and details the composition of medicines as well as the diseases and ailments for which such medicines are useful. Barbados is noted as an area where the "ass" or donkey is "bred" and where cotton and "guinea pepper" are grown; and in discussions of "Barbadoes nuts," aloes, gourds, and squashes, and their medicinal properties (pp. 293, 854, 873, 891, 907, 940, 941).

FOX, GEORGE
  A journal or historical account of the Life, Travels . . . of . . . George Fox.
  London, 1694-98. 2 vols.   [JCB, BL]
The Quaker leader lived in Barbados for three months during 1671. Volume 1 (pp. 351-61, 379) names various Barbados Quakers, and comments on the island's Quaker community, its social practices, the relationship between Quakers and non-Quakers (including the civil authorities), and includes the advice Fox gave Quakers for conducting themselves, including their relationships with slaves: slaves should be converted, treated "mildly and gently," and should be freed "after certain years of servitude"—radical preaching for the

period. Also included is an epistle written to Barbados Quakers in 1689 (pp. 599-600). A modern edition is briefly discussed in JSH-71.

THESAURUS GEOGRAPHICUS. A new body of geography.
  London, 1695. *506 pp.*   [JCB]
The Barbados section (pp. 488-89), based on sources which seem to include Ligon and Blome (see JSH-71, pp. 4, 8), includes an account of the island's discovery and early colonization, and describes its climate, flora and fauna, agricultural products, white and slave diets, religious establishment and church attendance, principal towns, bays, and caves.

CROESE, GERARD
  The general history of the Quakers.
  London, 1696. *276 pp.*   [JCB]
Barbados is mentioned as a place where persecuted English Quakers were shipped; incidents involving Quakers transported to the island as involuntary indentured servants are related (part 2, pp. 2, 12-14).

SLOANE, HANS
  Catalogus plantarum.
  London, 1696. *232 pp.*   [JCB]
Cited in JSH-71, but not described. This treatise of West Indian plant life, based on the observations of Sloane and others, is in Latin, although direct quotations from published sources are given in the original languages. Organized by plant type, the book frequently mentions Barbados. See also, James E. Dandy, *The Sloane Herbarium* (London: British Museum, 1958), for a number of references to plants from Barbados and the people who collected them.

FROGER, [FRANÇOIS]
  Relation d'un voyage fait en 1695, 1696, & 1697 aux cotes d'Afrique . . . & isles Antilles.
  Paris, 1698. *219 pp.*   [JCB]
The author's ship cruised the West Indies, attacking English shipping, in late 1696 and early 1697. Although he approached Barbados he never landed, but his work contains several brief entries which mention the island's military strength, give shipping and trading news (including imports from the Continental colonies), and English prizes taken. The English

translation, *A relation of a voyage made in the years 1695, 1696, 1697* (London, 1698 [JCB]), appears adequate although there are occasional (printing?) errors in various numbers and dates.

[CURSON, HENRY]
A compendium of the laws and government . . . of England . . . and dominions, plantations and territories thereunto pertaining . . . by H. C.
London, 1699. *642 pp.*   [JCB, BL]
The description of Barbados (pp. 527-30) may be derived entirely from Ligon (1657); it includes comments on physical geography and climate, first settlement, population, towns, and the governmental system. The JCB catalog identifies the author.

WAFER, LIONEL
A new voyage and description of the isthmus of America.
London, 1699. *224 pp.*   [JCB]
While sailing from Brazil in 1688 the author encountered Edwin Carter, "in a Barbadoes sloop," from whom he learned of King James's "proclamation to pardon and call in the buccaniers" (p. 223).

BARBADOS ASSEMBLY AND COUNCIL
An act to incourage privateers in case of a war.
[Boston? 1701?]. *Broadsheet.*   [HL]
Listed in JSH-71, but not consulted. Passed on November 18, 1701, this act emphasizes the important role played by "diverse privateers . . . from foreign parts" in defending Barbados. They "took several of the enemies vessels," but because of the high "charges and fees" demanded in condemning the prizes, and because British naval captains frequently pressed their men into the navy, privateers became discouraged and they all left Barbados. Thus the island's shipping was exposed "to the insults of His Majesties enemies" and Barbados was deprived of a "considerable addition of strength, which might have been hoped for from a good number of such privateers, had they been duly incouraged." Designed to remedy this situation, the act's final clause orders it to be "forthwith sent to New-England or some other convenient place to be printed." The only known copy is in the HL, whose catalog suggests the place of publication and gives 1701 as a provisional publication

date although the act may have been published in 1702. Available in the Evans microcard reprint series (No. 39370).

*BUGG, FRANCIS
The last will of that imposter Geo. Fox, the Quakers great apostle and admired idol.
London, 1701. *Broadside.*   [O-BO, LCP]
This "contains Josiah Coale's letter from Barbados" (*EA*). Locations and imprint data are given in *EA* and *ESTC*. See also, above, Coale 1671.

*GRAAF, NIKOLAAS DE
Reisen van Nicolaus de Graaff, na de vier gedeeltens des werelds, als Asia, Africa, America en Europa . . . d'Oost-Indise spiegel.
Hoorn, 1701. *225 pp.*   [LC, NYPL, BL]
A physician in the Dutch navy, Graaf spent five weeks in Barbados in 1649-53. His book, however, only relates (p. 30) the ordeal of a white servant, a teenager, who, while carrying two bottles of brandy to his master's plantation, tripped on a stone and was disemboweled by the broken glass when he fell. Carried to a neighboring house, he had his innards reinserted; later he removed them himself, cleaned them in milk, and ultimately recovered.

*PITTIS, WILLIAM
The true-born Englishman: a satyr answer'd.
London, 1701. *88 pp.*
This item in "prose and verse" mentions Barbados (p. 10) and other West Indian islands; copies are located at Harvard and Yale (*EA*, vol.5).

HODGES, THOMAS
The humble petition of Thomas Hodges Esq; to the honourable House of Commons, concerning the late male [sic]*-administration of justice in . . . . Barbadoes, and against the proceedings of the Council of Trade thereon. Delivered the 25th of Feburary 1701.*
[London, 1702]. *4 pp.*   [BL]
Complaints against Governor Grey, accusing him of negligence and delays with respect to his duties on the Court of Chancery and other Barbados courts; the petitioner had "several suits of considerable value" in the island's courts but because of Grey he lost a great deal of money. This rare item provides useful data on the operations of the island's judicial system.

PETIVER, JAMES

Gazophylacii naturae & artis decas prima.

London, 1702-06. *96 pp.* [BL]

This work by a celebrated British naturalist contains lists and brief notes on plants, shells, insects, etc., collected from various parts of the Old and New Worlds. The occasional references to Barbados materials sometimes include the names of the persons who sent or collected these materials, for example, William Stratton, James Ayrey, Thomas Walduck (see also JSH-71, p. 135).

BURCHETT, JOSIAH

Memoirs of transactions at sea during the war with France; beginning in 1688, and ending in 1697.

London, 1703. *408 pp.* [JCB]

A naval history, briefly mentioning Barbados in accounts of activities under captains Lawrence Wright in 1689, Ralph Wrenn in 1692, and Sir Francis Wheeler in 1692 (pp. 110-28, 168-73). References include instructions to the officers, arrival and departure dates, and comments on acquiring water and fresh food, crews, and military instructions and intelligence from Barbados's governor.

*GREAT BRITAIN, GENERAL POST OFFICE

Whereas Her Majesty, for the encouragement of trade and commerce, hath thought fit to appoint boats to convey letters . . . between England and the islands of Barbadoes, Antegoa . . . . This is to give notice, that a mail will go . . . on Thursday, the 25th of this instant february, . . . and thence forward, on the last thursday in every month.

[London, 1703]. [BL]

Citation and location from the *ESTC.*

[RIDPATH, GEORGE]

The case of Scots-men residing in England and in the English plantations.

Edinburgh, 1703. *14 pp.* [NL]

Argues that Scotsmen should have the same rights and privileges as Englishmen and that discrimination against them is detrimental to England's West Indian interests. Barbados is mentioned with respect to ships cleared for departure from the island that were seized or harassed because their owners or captains were

Scots; the role of Scots in the militia; the importation of over 2,000 Scottish servants. Author's name inscribed in manuscript in a contemporary hand on the title page.

AN ABRIDGEMENT of the laws in force and use in her majesty's plantations; (viz.) of Virginia, Jamaica, Barbadoes . . . etc. Digested under proper heads.

London, 1704. *495 pp.* [JCB, NYPL, NL]

The Barbados section of this rare work is pp. 181-284. The laws are abridged from Rawlin's *Laws of Barbados* (JSH-71) and are arranged by subject, for example, customs, elections, evidence, forcible entry, parishes. Each subject entry gives its related act and clause; this is very useful since Rawlin does not provide a subject index. Thus, the *Abridgement* permits reasonably ready access to Rawlin's main topics and specific subjects, although it is probably best used in conjunction with Rawlin.

MOLL, HERMAN

A new map of the island of Barbados.

London, 1708. [JCB]

Apparently based on Richard Ford's map of the 1670s (JSH-71, p. 9), and not on a survey, Moll's map identifies hundreds of Barbados's "principal plantations" and is published in the first edition (1708) of Oldmixon's *British Empire in America* (JSH-71); although later reprinted, its first appearance has been sometimes erroneously dated as 1717 (see E. M. Shilstone and T. Campbell in JSH-71, pp. 21, 103, 104).

TAYLOR, JOHN

An account of some of the labours, exercises, travels and perils . . . of John Taylor, of York.

London, 1710. *77 pp.* [BL, NYPL]

Mentioned in JSH-71, but not described. Taylor, a Quaker, first visited Barbados for a little over a month in 1659 and subsequently made about four other visits, the last in 1676; in all, he seems to have spent at least several months, if not longer, on the island. However, aside from observing the negative reactions he received to his preaching (he found the Barbadians "rude and uncivil, and some of them did thrust me out with violence"), he provides virtually no other details of his visits, not even the names of Quakers.

H.,T.
A short way to know the world; or the rudiments of geography.
London, 1712. 2nd ed. *234 pp.*   [BL]
In this superficial work, Barbados is barely mentioned in a brief discussion (pp. 220-21) of the Lesser Antilles.

*[HEYSHAM, ROBERT]
Observations, showing the great esteem had for the Royal African Company; with petitions of Robert Heysham (in 1693 and 1695) in behalf of his brothers, Giles and William Heysham in the island of Barbadoes.
[London?], 1712. *Broadside.*
Listed by Sabin (56577); a copy could not be found.

MOORE, JOHN
Of the truth and excellency of the gospel. A sermon preach'd before the Society for the Propagation of the Gospel in Foreign Parts . . . on Friday the 20th of February 1712/13.
London, 1713. *78 pp.*   [JCB]
Pages 1-47 contain Moore's sermon. Pages 49-78 are an "abstract" of the Society for the Propagation of the Gospel in Foreign Parts *Proceedings* for February 15, 1711/12 to February 20, 1712/13 (see JSH-71, p. 18), of which pp. 67-70 treat the Codrington plantations. During the year, Joseph Holt was appointed chaplain and catechist and charged with instructing the slaves in Christianity and supervising "the sick and maimed Negroes and servants." Holt's other duties are discussed, as are various aspects of the plantations' business affairs. There are also instructions to the Society's agents in Barbados with respect to plantation operations and slave management, and thanks to Colonel Christian Lilly for his architectural design of Codrington College.

STANHOPE, GEORGE
The early conversion of islanders, a wise expedient for propagating Christianity.
London, 1714. *55 pp.*   [JCB, BL]
Mostly a sermon, but includes "an abstract" of the Society for the Propagation of the Gospel in Foreign Parts *Proceedings* for 1712-13 (JSH-71, p. 18). The "abstract" includes (pp. 52-53) the SPG's activities in Barbados, particularly the proposal to construct Codrington College. Included also are drawings of the college by Colonel

Christian Lilly, an army engineer who had been stationed in Barbados where he had been involved in several major construction projects; his design of Codrington College was based on an Oxford college, but was later modified.

ZOUCH, [ARTHUR?]
Barbadoes. A catalogue of books, to be sold by Mr. Zouch .
[London? ca. 1715-16]. *35 pp.*   [LC]
Included in JSH-71, but not consulted. This rare item lists, mainly by short title and often only with the author's last name, approximately 780 published works arranged under fifteen heads, for example, law, dictionaries, poetry, voyages and travels, divinity, Greek and Roman history. Shows a considerable diversity of books available to the reading public of Barbados; only a very small number, however, deal with West Indian subjects. Internal evidence suggests the *Catalogue* was published no earlier than 1715-16; around this period, an Arthur Zouch was clerk of the Barbados Assembly and he may have been the bookseller. A photocopy is held by the JCB.

*[MAYO, WILLIAM]
[Prospectus for the publication of William Mayo's map A New and Exact Map of the island of Barbadoes].
[London], 1721. [*Broadside?*]   [PRO]
Title is my construction. E. M. Shilstone ("A descriptive list of maps of Barbados," *JBMHS*, 5, 1938, 66) reports the existence of this item, noting that a copy of it "is preserved in the Public Record Office." Shilstone cites the *Calendar of State Papers, Colonial Series, America and West Indies*, CO 28/17. In his article, he reproduces the text of the prospectus along with the royal license to publish this map; he also gives biographical details on Mayo. This well-known and important map of Barbados was published in London in 1722. Mentioned in JSH-71, but not consulted at the time, a copy of the map is located in the BL; another edition, with some minor differences from the BL copy (for example, the parishes are colored in yellow, green, and pink; the date of publication is not given; the title lacks the dates of the survey) is located in the NL.

THE PARTICULARS and inventories of the estates of the late sub-governor, deputy-governor, and directors of the South-Sea Company.
London, 1721. 2 vols.   [JCB, BL]
Each set of papers has its own title page and pagination. In volume 1 (pp. 3, 7) the papers of William Astell simply mention a "voyage from Barbados," while those of Robert Chester name about seventy-five of his debtors and creditors in Barbados, mention his interest in a ship bound for the island, provide financial details about his plantation (bought in 1707 from Joseph William and Thomas Skutt and sold in 1718 to Samuel Osborne), and horses he purchased from William Rawlins (pp. 1-8, 9, 10, 14, 15-34). In volume 2, the papers of William Morley mention Arthur P. Upton of Barbados in a list of creditors (p. 1) and those of Thomas Reynolds provide a few details regarding his royal grant as Barbados's Provost-Marshall (pp. 1, 23).

REYNOLDS, THOMAS
A sermon preach'd on the death of the Reverend Mr. William Hocker. With an account of his life.
London, 1722. *55 pp.*   [JCB, BL]
Hocker died in 1721, and in trying to illustrate the "goodness" of his character, Reynolds relates a story (p. 40) involving "a young gentlewoman from Barbados." Upon returning to Barbados from a visit to England, she and her mother (neither is named) were captured at sea and taken to Morocco. The two women were "stript of all they had," but the daughter managed to hide "a manuscript of Christian counsel and advice" she had received from Hocker before she left England. The mother was freed after several years and, upon returning to England, "declar'd of how great use that small piece of Mr. Hocker's was both to her and her daughter in their affliction." The daughter was apparently never freed, and was compelled to join the sultan's harem.

ROBERTS, GEORGE
The four years voyages of Captain George Roberts.
London, 1726. *458 pp.*   [BL]
Included in JSH-71, where it was assumed that Roberts was the author and his account factual. Now it is generally accepted as one of Daniel Defoe's fictional works that he assembled from newspapers

and other contemporary sources; see M. Schonhorn, "*Defoe's* Four Years Voyages of Capt. George Roberts *and* Ashton's Memorial" (*Texas Studies in Literature and Language* 17, 1975,93-102).

[HALLEY, EDMUND] (Ed.)
Miscellanea curiosa.
London, 1726-27. 3rd ed. 3 vols.
[JCB, BL]
Records wind conditions in Barbados (vol. 1, p. 95).

WOODWARD, JOHN
Fossils of all kinds.
London, 1728. *131 pp.*   [BL, H]
A brief discussion of "Barbadoes-tar" (p. 38), based on Ligon (1657), notes its similarity to "petroleum" found in springs of England and Scotland.

COLMAN, BENJAMIN
The faithful ministers of Christ mindful of their own death. A sermon preached . . . in Boston; upon the death of . . . Solomon Stoddard.
Boston, 1729. *29 pp.*   [H]
Contains an obituary (pp. 26-29) of Stoddard, a well-known New England clergyman, which first appeared in the *Boston Weekly News-letter*, February 13, 1729. The obituary briefly mentions that, for reasons of health, Stoddard went to Barbados where he served as chaplain to Governor Searle and "preach'd to dissenters," returning to New England "in about two years." At present, there are no known manuscripts written by Stoddard relating to his sojourn in Barbados from around 1667 to 1669.

GEE, JOSHUA
The trade and navigation of Great Britain considered.
London, 1729. *145 pp.*   [JCB]
Argues that Britain can best increase its wealth and employment by preventing imports of goods that can be raised or manufactured at home or in the colonies. Barbados is occasionally mentioned (pp. 20, 45, 59), including the comment that it "is very much worn out, and does not afford the quantity of sugars as heretofore, and yet the planters live in great splendor and at vast expence." References to Barbados in later editions (London, 1730, 1731, 1738 [JCB]) appear to be the same.

A COMPARISON between the British sugar colonies and New England, as they relate to the interest of Great Britain.
London, 1732. *43 pp.*   [BL, JCB]
Deals with economic and trade issues. The author emphasizes the actual and potential value of the West Indies to Great Britain and argues that if economically protected, the former can continue to be of great value to the latter while "the present advantage" of New England "in all probability will, in a few years, be quite lost." Barbados is mentioned in several places to illustrate particular points.

KEIMER, SAMUEL
The sorrowful lamentation of Samuel Keimer, printer of the Barbados Gazette. Barbados Gazette, May 4, 1734.
This poem, reproduced in Isaiah Thomas (vol. 2 [1810], pp. 387-88), originally appeared in the *Barbados Gazette*, May 4, 1734, and apparently was never published separately. There is no known copy of this issue of the *Gazette*, and the poem was not published in Keimer's *Caribbeana* (see JSH-71). Addressed "to those wou'd-be thought gentlemen, who have long taken this paper, and never paid for it, and seem never to design to pay for it," the first four lines are: "What a pity it is that some modern bravadoes/ Who dub themselves gentlemen here in Barbadoes/ Should time after time, run in debt to their printer/And care not to pay him in summer or winter!"

SNELGRAVE, WILLIAM
A new account of some parts of Guinea, and the slave-trade.
London, 1734. *288 pp.*   [H]
This well-known account by an English slaver includes a few brief references to Barbados in connection with his slaving voyages, suicides among "Cormantine Negroes" (pp. 173, 202, 266), and in the story (pp. 67-72) of an English slave trader who made an agreement with the King of Dahomey; by violating that agreement the English slave trade along that part of the African coast was potentially threatened.

* A PASTORAL lamenting the death of . . . Scroope Lord Viscount Howe, Governour of Barbados and late member of parliament for the county of Nottingham.
Cambridge [Eng.], 1736. *20 pp.*   [URB]
Citation and location from *ESTC*; another copy is at the University of Cincinnati.

Although the ESTC lists a copy at the BL, a search at the BL with the librarians failed to yield one, indicating that the only known copies are in U.S. repositories.

BARBADOS. JOHN Burke merchant and Elizabeth his wife—appellants. Martha Lane widow, Mary Lane widow, Robert Burnett, gent. and Mary his wife. The case of the appellants, John Burke and his wife.
[London, 1738].   [JCB]

. . . THE CASE of the appellant Mary Lane, and who is also respondent in the several appeals of John Burke and his wife, and of Robert Burnett and his wife.
[London, 1738].   [JCB]

. . . THE CASE of the appellants Robert Burnett and Mary his wife, and who are also respondents in the several appeals of Mary Lane and John Burke and Elizabeth his wife.
[London, 1738].   [JCB]

. . . THE CASE of the respondent Martha Lane, the widow and executrix of John Lane only (and who was sole plaintiff below) to all the said three appeals.
[London, 1738].   [JCB]
Four separately printed legal briefs, each of four folio pages with its own pagination; all four are bound together in the JCB. This complicated case, interwoven with a history of intrafamily conflict among heirs, involves the repercussions of monetary loans made in the first decade or so of the eighteenth century by Ann Nevinson, who owned land and slaves in Barbados, to Anthony Lane, an island merchant and her brother-in-law. Both were deceased at the time of the case. Heard before the Lords of the Privy Council in London in March 1738, the appellants ask for a reversal of a decision made by the Court of Chancery in Barbados in August 1737; the respondent asks that the 1737 decision be upheld and the appellants' case be dismissed. In a judgment written in manuscript on the first of the above listed items, the Privy Council decides for a reversal of the 1737 decision. The relationships among the parties are: Elizabeth Burke and Mary Burnett are sisters and the only children of Anthony Lane; they are also the nieces of Ann Nevinson who is the sister of Anthony's second wife, Mary Lane. Martha Lane is Mary's sister-in-law and the widow of John Lane, Anthony's younger brother.

*RAWLIN, WILLIAM

Case of William Rawlin, searcher of His Majesty's entries and customs at Bridge Town, Barbadoes, and Henry Warren, doctor of physic, in the island.

[London], 1738.

Two items: the appellant's case and the respondent's case. Listed in the bookseller Henry Stevens's catalog *Rare Americana* (London, 1927, p. 529) which states this item concerns "the seizure of a consignment of sugar not properly described for duty." The catalog also reports that this is one of several "West India cases [that] were privately printed for the use of interested parties only, and are consequently very rare." I have been unable to locate a copy.

CHARNOCK, BENJAMIN

Barbadoes, Benjamin Charnock of . . . Barbadoes, esq. appelant; Elliot Saer, of the same island, esq. and George Gascoijne, respondents.

[London], 1738. *4 pp.*   [JCB]

Submitted to the Privy Council in London, this brief seeks final disposal of a case involving a land transaction in Barbados; the original judgment had been handed down in 1718. Thomas Maxwell and William Ramsay were the other principals involved in this case.

BELL, JOHN

An epistle to friends in Maryland, Virginia, Barbadoes, and the other colonies, and islands in the West-Indies, where any Friends are.

London, 1741. *4 pp.*   [JCB, NYPL]

Included in JSH-71, but not consulted. Addressed to slaveholders, the epistle discusses how they should treat their slaves by, for example, "carefully avoiding all oppression in extream labour, severe chastisement, or with-holding . . . sufficient subsistence of meat, drink, and cloathing . . . ." Aside from the names in the title, there are no specific references to any territory.

*BROME, WILLIAM

Case of William Brome, son and heir of Samuel Brome of the island of Barbadoes, and Sir John Eyles.

[London], 1741.

See next entry.

*BROWNE, SUSANNA AND WILLIAM

Case of Susanna and William Browne and Sir John Eyles.

[London], 1741.

Both preceding titles were obtained from the Henry Stevens catalog *Rare Americana* (London, 1927, p. 529) which reports these as "West India cases [that] were privately printed for the use of interested parties only." Copies of neither could be located.

[HEATH, C. A.?]

Considerations against laying any new duty upon sugar; wherein is particularly shewn, that a new imposition will be ruinous to the sugar colonies . . . and greatly conducive to the aggrandizement of France.

London, 1744. *36 pp.*   [LC, BL]

Major arguments are summarized in the title; occasional references to Barbados illustrate specific points. There is no indication that the author had spent any time in the Caribbean; he is tentatively identified in the BL catalog. A 1746 edition was published under the title *Considerations relating to a new duty upon sugar* (Sabin 102826).

INGRAM, DALE

An essay, on the nature, cause and seat of dysentery's, in a letter to Dr. Henry Warren of Barbados . . .

Barbados [1744]. *61 pp.*   [O-TR]

This rare item is mentioned in JSH-71 (p. 32) under a somewhat different title, but had not been located. Ingram practiced medicine in Barbados at least during the 1740s; he was also a "professor at Codrington College" (*JBMHS*, 21, 1953, 21). His book, a purely medical thesis, was prompted by the prevalence of dysentery on the island. Although he notes the high mortality rates this "tyrant" caused and implies its particular devastation to slaves, he gives no information on how Barbadians specifically reacted to the disease, local cures employed, etc. The preface is dated Barbados, February 1743-44, and a contemporary manuscript notation on the title page gives 1744 as the year of publication. Published by William Beeby, this is among the earliest items known to have been printed in Barbados.

JOURNAL OF the expedition to La Guira and
Porto Cavallos in the West-Indies, under the
command of Commodore Knowles. In a letter
from an officer on board the Burford to his
friend in London.
London, 1744. *63 pp.*   [JCB]
Detailed account of a British naval/military
expedition against Spanish settlements in
Venezuela. The author's ship came from
St. Kitts, and although one or a few of the
vessels came from Barbados (p. 58), there
is no information on the latter.

SMITH, WILLIAM
    A new voyage to Guinea.
London, 1744. *279 pp.*   [BL]
After completing a tour of coastal West
Africa for the Royal African Company,
Smith's ship develops a serious leak on its
return voyage to England. Heading for
Barbados, "we anchor'd safe in Carlisle
Bay" on July 16, 1727, and stayed for about
a month while the ship was repaired.
Although the author "took my pleasure
ashore upon that rich fertile, and well
inhabited island," he felt no need to
provide a description of Barbados since it
is "already so well known to most
Europeans, from the many and true
accounts of it by others." The few pages on
Barbados (pp. 272-275) mainly describe
the repairs made to the ship.

HUSBANDS, RICHARD
    *Barbados. By his excellency's command.
    Whereas a provisional treaty hath lately been
    concluded betwixt . . .*
[Barbados, 1749]. *Broadside.*   [HL]
Interleaved among the Grenville papers
(STG, Box 24, no. 29), this rare item is
signed at the end "Richard Husbands,

Deputy Secretary" and dated "Secretary's
Office, December 18, 1749." This "publick
notice," presumably posted or distributed
in Barbados and ordered by Governor
Henry Grenville, announces the signing of
a treaty between Grenville and the French
governor of Martinique concerning "the
reciprocal evacuation" of Tobago until
there is a more definitive agreement on
the claims of England and France to that
island. The governors agreed that neither
nation should colonize Tobago, but that
both would be permitted access to the
island "to wood, water, and fish" and could
build temporary shelters "while wooding or
fishing"; no one, however, was to establish
farms, cut timber, other than firewood, or
collect "rare and medicinal plants and
other valuable vegetables."

TABAGO: OR, a geographical description,
natural and civil history.
London [1749]. *89 pp.*   [JCB]
Occasional references to Barbadian
connections with Tobago during the
seventeenth century; based on unspecified
sources.

[GRENVILLE, HENRY]
    Barbados. December 18th 1750.
[Barbados? 1750]. *Broadsheet.*   [HL].
Interleaved among the Grenville papers
(STG, Box 25, no. 29), this contains an
address by Governor Grenville to the
Barbados Council and Assembly
concerning a "new excise bill" and the
need for repairing and maintaining the
island's fortifications; also replies by the
Council and Assembly and the governor's
response to the replies.

1751-1800

ALLEN, HENRY
    *Dissertatio medica inauguralis de fluoris albi
    charactere et notis, quibus cum gonorrhaea
    convenit vel differt et utriusquecuratione etc.*
Leiden, 1751. *22 pp.*   [JCB]
A medical dissertation, by a Barbadian, on
the "white flux" and its similarities and
dissimilarities to gonorrhea, with a
suggested cure for each; dedicated to the
author's father, Robert Allen. Contains no
information on Barbados.

BEAWES, WYNDHAM
    *Lex mercatoria rediviva: or, the merchant's
    directory.*
London [1751]. *922 pp.*   [JCB]
Includes a very brief and superficial
account (pp. 664-65), based on various
sources, of Barbados's early history,
economic state, produce, and trade. Other
editions include: Dublin (1754), and
several published in London (1761, 1783,
1792) [BL].

FOTHERGILL, JOHN
An account of the life and travels in the work of the ministry of John Fothergill.
London, 1753. *357 pp.*   [BL]
An English Quaker who spent about six months in Barbados on three separate visits, in 1705 or 1706, in 1723-24, and in 1737-38—the last two visits when the island's Quaker community, once relatively numerous, had declined considerably. Fothergill briefly records his visits and attendance at Quaker meetings. Although he occasionally mentions the names of resident Quakers, he says very little about Barbados or its Quaker community (pp. 50-51, 184-86, 190-92, 283-84, 290-92). Also included in this volume are two epistles written from Barbados (pp. 192-207, 284-90).

Fothergill played an important role in the decision of Dr. William Hillary, a fellow Quaker, to establish a practice in Barbados (see above, Hillary 1759).

POOLE, ROBERT
The beneficient bee: or, traveller's companion. Containing each day's observation, in a voyage from London, to Gibraltar, Barbadoes, Antigua, Barbuda, Mountserrat, Nevis . . . . Containing a summary account of the said places.
London, 1753. *388 pp.*   [BL, HL].
Leaving England in October, 1748, Poole, a British medical doctor, arrived at Barbados in December, 1748, and departed in March, 1749. His account of Barbados, in almost one hundred double-columned pages of small print (pp. 207-305), is unusually lengthy for an eighteenth-century traveler, and offers a relatively rich array of observations on the island. Poole lived in Bridgetown but made frequent excursions into the countryside and visited many parts of the island from St. Lucy to St. Philip. Barbados, he observed, "is so everywhere furnished with inhabitants, that it much resembles a scattered village in the midst of a garden."

Poole's comments (varying from brief to lengthy) are on a wide variety of topics. Considerable space is devoted to descriptions of fruits, vegetables, and other plants (with occasional references to Griffith Hughes's book [1750; see JSH-71]), including occasional information on medicinal use of plants. Agricultural practices are recorded, particularly sugar cane cultivation and grinding mechanisms, and sugar and rum manufacture are described. There are also detailed daily notes on the weather, many observations on the white creoles (for example, their mannerisms, dress, diets, hospitality, houses and house furnishings), and slave treatment and slave life (such as, punishments and cruelties against them, music, marketing, holidays, dress, housing, funerals, diets, obeah). Observations are also made on whitewashing of houses, booksellers and printers, locally made beverages, currency, shipping in Carlisle Bay, notification of arriving vessels and legal procedures for leaving the island, Christmas and its manner of celebration, insects (particularly ants, termites, and chiggers), land crabs, rats, and diseases. Comments are offered on population and demographic issues, the militia, governmental and judicial systems, Bridgetown (architecture, streets, and taverns), and Needham's fort and Oistins. There are geographical descriptions of the Barbadian countryside and the Scotland District, with comments on, for example, the road system, Cole's Cave, Barbados Tar, Porey Spring, Codrington College, and the Animal Flower Cave in St. Lucy (a lengthy account). Descriptions are also given of the parish churches of St. Philip, Christ Church, and St. Michael, and there is a description of Governor Henry Grenville's procession to attend church on Sunday,

From Barbados, Poole went to Antigua and other British Leeward islands (pp. 306 ff.); comparative comments on Barbados are also interspersed among his comments on these islands.

[CHALKLEY, THOMAS]
Youth persuaded to obedience, gratitude, and honour to God, and their parents . . .written at sea . . . September, 1730.
Newcastle Upon Tyne, 1754. *23 pp.* [JCB]
Sabin (11753) lists a 1730 Barbados edition which was cited in JSH-71, but no copy could be located. The 1754 edition has a 1730 date printed on each page with the initials T. C printed at the end; it contains no references to Barbados.

BELGROVE, WILLIAM
A treatise upon husbandry or planting.
Boston, 1755. *86 pp.*   [BL, JCB, H]
Described in JSH-71, but recent information sheds light on some relevant

bibliographic issues (see chapter 3, Oxford University, Rawlinson Mss. A. 348).

[MCCULLOH, HENRY]

A miscellaneous essay concerning the courses pursued by Great Britain in the affairs of her colonies.

London, 1755. *134 pp.*   [JCB]

Treats trade and politics, chiefly of the mainland colonies; occasionally, however, the West Indies, including Barbados, is mentioned. For authorship, see Sabin 43122, 43123.

VOOGT, CLAAS JANSZ

De nieuwe groote lichtende zee-fakkel, 't vierde deel.

[Amsterdam, ca. 1755].   [JCB]

A large atlas containing thirty-four maps of the New World. The Barbados map ("Nieuwe land en zeekaart van het eyland Barbados geleegen in West India") is 23 by 21 inches and is clearly a somewhat modified copy of Richard Ford's ca. 1675 map (JSH-71, p. 9). Although the interior details of both maps seem to be identical (with some variations in font style for some locations), major differences exist in the decorative features outside the body of the maps: the art work of the Ford map is absent from the Dutch one, and the latter contains a description of Barbados which is much shorter (and differs somewhat in content) than the Ford map description. The most significant difference, however, is that the Dutch map contains two insets: a detail of Carlisle Bay and neighboring areas of Bridgetown (with named forts and plantations); and topographic profiles of Barbados as seen from different approaches at sea.

A GENUINE account of the late secret expedition to Martinico and Guardaloupe [sic], *under Commodore Moore and General Hopson.*

London, 1759. *23 pp.*   [JCB]

"Written by a Sea-Officer who went out with Commodore Hughes," the fleet arrived at Barbados on 3 January 1759, taking on fresh water, carrying out military maneuvers, and ultimately acquiring "a number of Negroes for drawing the artillery, etc." Although "promised a body of volunteers . . . they were never sent," and on 13 January 1759 the fleet of about seventy-five ships left Barbados for Martinique; one of the warships was fitted out as a "hospital-ship" and carried

"surgeons, or such as called themselves so," who "were hired from Bridgetown" (pp. 4-5).

HILLARY, WILLIAM

Observations on the changes of the air and the concomitant epidemical diseases in the island of Barbadoes.

London, 1759. *373 pp.*   [JCB]

The first edition of a book whose second edition was published in London in 1766 (JSH-71). Due to erroneous information in Sabin, JSH-71 lists the first edition as published in 1754; a nonexistent 1752 edition, mentioned by Frank Cundall (*Bibliography of the West Indies, Excluding Jamaica* [Kingston, Jamaica, 1909]) was also reported (JSH-71 p. 35). For biographical details on Hillary, especially his twelve-year residence in Barbados in the 1740s and 1750s, and for corroborative information on various editions of his *Observations* ("one of the first treatises . . . by an English physician which deals specifically with tropical diseases"), see C. C. Booth, "William Hillary, a pupil of Boerhaave" (*Medical History*, 7, 1963, 297-316).

J., J.

Candid reflections on the expedition to Martinico. With an account of the taking of Guadaloupe by General Barrington.

London, 1759. *50 pp.*   [JCB, NYPL]

Identifying himself as naval lieutenant, the author apparently did not participate in the events he describes. Barbados is briefly mentioned (pp. 2-3) with respect to the provisioning and watering of the fleet, military maneuvers, and the acquisition of "about 300 Negroes for drawing the artillery"; seventy-five ships ultimately left Barbados for Martinique.

MASSIE, JOSEPH

A state of the British sugar-colony trade . . . submitted to the consideration of the honourable House of Commons.

London, 1759. *40 pp.*   [JCB]

A detailed discussion of trade with the sugar colonies, such as slave labor costs and sugar production, which argues that the British duty on unrefined sugar can be increased without making sugar more expensive in Britain and without "distressing the British sugar-planters." Contains occasional references to Barbados, but no indication that the author had visited the island.

MASSIE, JOSEPH
Calculations and observations relating to an additional duty upon sugar.
Westminister, 1759. *Broadsheet.* [JCB, HL]
Published separately from Massie's *A state of the British sugar-colony trade*, this item was originally intended to be included with it. The *Calculations*, which is bound into the JCB copy of Massie's book, details the costs of producing muscovado sugar in the British colonies and discusses such topics as cane production per acre, sugar yields per land unit, etc. Barbados is sometimes mentioned.

[WALKER, GEORGE]
The voyages and cruises of Commodore Walker, during the late Spanish and French Wars.
London, 1760. 2 vols. [JCB]
Volume 1 (p. 13) briefly mentions that the ship *Duke William*, sometimes a privateer and captained and co-owned by Walker, stayed four months in Barbados in 1742 loading cargo; it sailed in October accompanied by "the captains Staples, Chambers, and Burrows, who put themselves under our convoy." The *Duke William* was lost at sea during a hurricane on the return voyage to England. The JCB catalog identifies the author.

BLENMAN, WILLIAM
The case of Jonathan Blenman, Esq. Attorney-General of Barbadoes, etc. Humbly submitted by his son, William Blenman.
London, 1761. *8 pp.* [BL]
A rare item, bound into a volume of manuscripts (Additional mss. 32921, no. 27). Blenman's son defends his father from charges against him by John Moore, the British naval commander of Barbados and the Leeward islands, and requests the king to renew the senior Blenman's commission as Attorney-General of Barbados, a position he had held for thirty-five years, which had been held up because of Moore's "formal complaint" against him. The complaint relates to incidents during 1760, involving trade with neighboring islands, and with accusations that Blenman infringed on the interests and authority of the British naval establishment; there is also evidence of great personal acrimony between Moore and Blenman. A useful item for issues of trade as well as Barbadian relations with the British navy.

GREAT BRITAIN, PARLIAMENT
An act for vesting the plantation and estate of John Walter, esquire, and Newton his wife (late Newton Walker, spinster) in the island of Barbadoes, in trustees, for raising money to be applied in purchasing of stock, and for other purposes for the improvement of the same plantation and estate.
[London, 1761]. *11 pp.* [BL, CU]
A private act (no. 42 in a volume of 1761 private bills, located in the Offical Publication Library) that concerns Mount Wilton, a plantation of about seven hundred acres; aside from names in the title, others include Newton Walter, Abell Walter, Abell Dottin, Elisha Biscoe, and Alexander Walker.

HUGHES, SYLVIA
The adventures of Sylvia Hughes. Written by herself.
London, 1761. *230 pp.* [NL, BL]
A rambling autobiographical narrative in which the narrator/heroine falls in love with a young man who spends three years in Barbados. Upon his return to England, he provides a brief account of the island (pp. 219-27) which mentions hurricanes, the preparation of cassava bread, fishing techniques, geographical features, the Animal Flower Cave, chiggers, and various types of flora and their uses. This account, however, does not appear to be based on the author's own experiences. To the reading public for which this novel was intended, Barbados "is generally esteem'd the Garden of the West-Indies. It is a place of much trade, and great advantages arise to the inhabitants from it, which induces many persons to quit happier climates and settle there." A facsimile edition was published by the Garland Publishing Company (New York and London, 1975).

REASONS AGAINST the renewal of the sugar act, as it will be prejudicial to the trade, not only of the northern colonies, but to that of Great-Britain also.
Boston, 1764. *19 pp.* [JCB]
Argues that renewing duties on "foreign" sugar and molasses entering the British colonies will adversely affect the trade and commerce of Massachusetts. Details are given on the Massachusetts fishing industry, New England's consumption of molasses and rum and its trade with the West Indies. Contains materials implicitly relevant to Barbados although the island is

only specifically mentioned once: vessels trading from New England to the West Indies (except those bound directly for Surinam or Jamaica) usually go first to Barbados "to try the market" and then proceed to other British colonies, and, if need be, "other foreign islands" (p. 18).

[YOUNG, WILLIAM]

Considerations which may tend to promote the settlement of our new West-India colonies, by encouraging individuals to embark in the undertaking.

London, 1764. *49 pp.*   [JCB]

In arguing for the economic advantages that could accrue to colonizers of Grenada, Dominica, St. Vincent, and Tobago, there are a few minor references to Barbados "the most windward, best peopled, and most powerful of any of our sugar colonies." The second edition, *Some observations; which may contribute to afford a just idea of the nature, importance, and settlement, of our New West-India colonies* (London, 1764), is similar to *Considerations* and contains some of its passages, but has some new materials, a different collation, and different organization; it also contains a few additional minor references to Barbados. Author attribution is in the JCB catalog and Sabin (106126).

[FOTHERGILL, JOHN]

Considerations relative to the North American colonies.

London, 1765. *48 pp.*   [BL]

In an effort to convey the character and importance of the North American colonists and colonies, there are occasional comparisons to the West Indies in general, but only one specific reference to Barbados and the potential value of its agricultural acreage.

ASSOCIATES OF DOCTOR BRAY

An account of the designs of the associates of the late Dr Bray; with an abstract of their proceedings.

London, 1766. *47 pp.*   [JCB]

The one reference to Barbados (p. 19), notes that an unspecified number of books, valued at £5, was sent to the island "to lay the foundation of parochial libraries in the several parishes." The same statement is made in a later report with the same title (London, 1794, p. 15 [JCB]).

BENEZET, ANTHONY

A caution and warning to Great Britain and her colonies, in a short representation of the calamitous state of the enslaved Negroes in the British Dominions.

Philadelphia, 1766. *35 pp.*   [JCB]

Extracted materials taken from various sources on the subject of slavery. The few brief references to Barbados (pp. 5, 7, 29-30) are taken from published sources and include the Quaker leader George Fox's words, spoken in Barbados in 1671, stressing more liberal treatment for slaves.

CHALKLEY, THOMAS

A collection of the works of . . . Thomas Chalkley.

London, 1766. 4th ed. *580 pp.*   [JCB]

The first edition (Philadelphia, 1749) is discussed in JSH-71, but had not been consulted. The initial portion of this work (pp. 1-326) is Chalkley's autobiography, written toward the end of his life in 1741. Between 1701 and 1735, Chalkley, a Quaker merchant from Pennsylvania, visited Barbados about seventeen times (mostly from 1727 to 1735), visits ranging in duration from three weeks to three and a half months—a total of about two and a half years on the island. (A longer version of the 1718 visit exists in manuscript and was published in the *JBMHS*; see JSH-71, p. 33.)

Most of the pages dealing with these visits provide few details on Barbados or its Quaker community, and briefly, often very superficially, mention his activities, for example, attendance at meetings and funerals ("this island . . . indeed doth prove a grave to many new-comers"), and visits to the sick; occasionally the names of Quakers whom he stayed with or encountered; the houses or places where meetings took place, or the number of meeting houses. Sometimes no details on a visit are given; he simply reports he attended meetings. Occasionally there are brief comments on other matters relating to Barbados: a 1707 encounter at sea with a privateer while approaching the island; a severe drought and a cloud of volcanic ashes over Barbados in 1717-18; Barbadian whites and their behavior; types of locally made "cool drinks"; Oliver's cave in 1717-18; market and trading conditions in Bridgetown in 1718; earthquake tremors in Speightstown in 1727; visits with Governor Henry Worsley; a hurricane in mid-1730 and another in mid-1731, including the damage caused; in 1735, an epidemic killed "near twenty masters of vessels and some hundreds of people."

Slavery is only mentioned twice: in one place, Chalkley implies that slaves attended at least one of his meetings, and he preached on the subject during his last and longest visit (three and a half months in 1735). At a "very large meeting" attended by "many" non-Quakers he preached on "charity" and advised them to "shew it forth to all people . . . and also to their Negroes, telling them that some of the gentry of this island had observed to me that the more kind they were to their slaves, they had their business the better done for it." However, "in divers houses, and some of note, I could not hear any Christian-like expressions to their slaves or Negroes, and . . . with sorrow I had seen a great deal of tyranny and cruelty, to which I disswaded them from; this doctrine so exasperated some . . . that they made a disturbance at the meeting; one of which persons meeting me on the King's High-way, shot off his fowling-piece at me, being loaded with small shot, ten of which made marks on me, and several drew blood" (pp. 33-275, passim; pp. 116-18 are an epistle written in 1724 to Barbados Quakers.

The remainder of the *Collection* (pp. 327-580) is "The Works of that Ancient, faithful servant of Jesus Christ, Thomas Chalkley"; includes his epistles and other writings, compiled after his death.

During his 1735 trip, the Friends in Barbados "published a little piece I wrote at sea, which I called *Free Thoughts Communicated to Free Thinkers,* done in order to promote thinking on the name and works of God" (JSH-71, p. 28).

[STEELE, JOSHUA]

An account of a late conference on the occurrences in America. In a letter to a friend.
London, 1766. *40 pp.* [JCB]
A table lists the English colonies in North America and the West Indies, including Barbados, by their estimated population and the amount of sterling each "contributed to the general fund or public revenue" of Great Britain (p. 40). The author's name is inscribed in a contemporary manuscript hand on the title page of the JCB copy.

AN AFFECTING relation of the appearance of Thomas Ostrehan's apparition, to his friend Robert Straker . . . being an extract of a letter from a gentleman in Barbados to his friend in Philadelphia, dated November 1766.
Philadelphia, 1767. *8 pp.* [BL]
This rare and anonymously authored item narrates an event that was supposed to have occurred in Barbados. Ostrehan and Straker, "two youths of this island," were close friends since their school days in England, continuing this friendship after their return to Barbados. Ostrehan "lately died" and on the night after his funeral his ghost appeared in Straker's bedroom, telling him of dangers that were to befall Straker's brother and urging him to warn his father of these dangers; also predicting that he, Straker, will "shortly die" and "another of our schoolmates will soon follow." The ghost's predictions came to pass. The author of this pamphlet received this account "from an intimate friend in Straker's family, to whom the affair was communicated by them."

HOLST, MATTHIAS
An almanack for the island of Barbados, for the year . . . 1769.
London [1768]. *Broadside.* [JCB]
A sheet almanac containing standard almanac information; also the names of the Barbados Council and judges of the island's courts. Published by H. Woodfall "for Matthias Holst, and sold by him at his house in Broad-Street, Bridgetown," this may have been compiled by John Dolland, and is one of an apparently rare series which started around 1755 and continued for at least thirty-five years (see JSH-71, pp. 36-37, 50).

KEELING, JOSEPH
The case of Joseph Keeling, Esq; relative to his claim to a large estate in the island of Barbados.
[London, 1768]. *4 pp.* [BL]
A rare document relating to the Rawdon plantation in St. Michael. Between 1654 and 1665 this 300-acre plantation had belonged to Thomas Rawdon. In 1665, he left Barbados and subdivided the plantation, giving ninety-nine year leases to about thirty different tenants. Joseph Keeling had married a female heir of Rawdon and was laying claim to the original 300-acre estate, and the rents that

it brought, since the leases had expired in 1764. Thwarted by several of the original tenants' descendants, Keeling first sent his agent from England to Barbados to press his claims, but then was forced to go to the island himself. An interesting case reflecting the mechanics and nature of Barbados's judicial and legal system.

THOMPSON, EDWARD

Sailor's letters. Written to his select friends in England, during his voyages and travels in Europe, Asia, and America from the year 1754 to 1759.

Dublin, 1770. *178 pp.*   [JCB]

As a British naval lieutenant, the author was on duty in the West Indies in late 1756 and early 1757. One of his letters, dated Barbados, December 5, 1756 (pp. 112-14) summarizes a several weeks stay on the island; it includes brief comments on Bridgetown, the cost of goods ("everything is dear but flying fish"), the white creoles ("more easy, hospitable, and kind than on the other islands, but yet have that volatile spirit so peculiar to the creole"), and the treatment of slaves. He witnessed a white woman torturing her slave who had "committed some trivial domestic error," and comments on the "planter's ladies" and their cruelty toward slaves "for they are taught in their very infancy to flog with a whip the slave that offends them." There are also brief comments on slave curing practices, obeah, and their magico-religious beliefs. Reflecting on his West Indian experiences prior to departure, Thompson gives a relatively lengthy characterization of white creoles, including Barbadians, "a volatile, haughty, ignorant people; fond of dress, pomp and pageantry, and slaves to all the *cardinal vices* . . . . The women, in general, unhappily cherish a low pride. Few are acquainted with good breeding, and more unacquainted with modesty. Swearing in a vulgar corruped dialect at their slaves in general . . . and ogling and intriguing no where more common; which in a great measure may be attributed to the men, who carry on amours with their ladies slaves, and the less private, the more *degagé* and genteel" (pp. 125-26).

First published in London in 1766, a "second edition corrected" was also published in London in 1767 (BL).

GUTHRIE, WILLIAM

A new geographical, historical, and commercial grammar.

London, 1771. 2nd ed. 2 vols.   [BL]

Volume 2 (pp. 428-29) contains a brief and conventional overview of Barbados's geography, early history, and colonization, economy, population, and agricultural products. Based on various sources, including Ligon (1657). The first American edition (Philadelphia, 1794-95), titled *A new system of modern geography,* treats Barbados in vol. 2, pp. 613-14 [JCB].

BELLIN, JACQUES NICOLAS

L'hydrographie Françoise recuil des cartes générales et particulieres qui ont été faites pour le service des vaisseaux du roy, par ordre des Ministres de la Marine depuis1737, jusqu'en 1765.

Paris, 1772. 2 vols.   [JCB]

Volume 2 includes engraved maps of Africa and America with all geographical features and descriptive materials in French. The Barbados map, 55.5 x 40.2 cm, primarily shows coastal features; its inset reads "Carte de l'isle de la Barbade . . . . MDCCLVIII . . . avec une description géographique de cette isle." The geographical description was published separately (JSH-71, p. 36). See also T. Campbell, *The Printed Maps of Barbados,* The Map Collectors' Circle (London, 1965).

MANTE, THOMAS

The history of the late war in North-America, and the islands of the West-Indies.

London, 1772. *542 pp.*   [LC, BL]

Describes the British fleet's arrival in Carlisle Bay in January 1759, and reports on such activities as watering the ships, landing and reembarking troops, trying to find volunteers, and recruiting slaves; many troops died in Barbados because of a smallpox epidemic, but about 6,000 men ultimately left the island to confront the French (pp. 163-65). Admiral Rodney arrived at Barbados in November 1761, and the Barbados government raised 500 whites and 600 blacks to accompany his expedition; also given are the names and types of ships (with the number of men on each), the names of land force units and their commanders, etc., that sailed under Rodney's command for Martinique (pp. 348-49, 351-52). The author may have been involved in the events and activities he describes.

[ORDERSON, JOHN?]
[Extracts from the *Barbados Mercury*, 1772-1773].
[Barbados? ca. 1773-74]. ca. *200 pp.*
[NYHS]
Contains extracts of various lengths from the *Barbados Mercury* newspaper, including: minutes of the Assembly and the Court of Grand Sessions; letters to the editor on internal, particularly political, affairs; literary pieces and poetry; brief essays on philosophical, political, agricultural, and economic subjects; also occasional obituaries and death notices; reprinting of articles from other West Indian newspapers, and descriptions of social events in Barbados's white community.

The NYHS copy lacks the title page, thus making the title as well as author, place, and date of publication conjectural; the first four pages of the volume are also missing. Pagination starts at p. 5 and continues through consecutively numbered pages to p. 192; the original volume clearly had additional pages, but probably not many more. Although the date of the first entry is on the missing front pages, it was probably Saturday, October 17 or Saturday, October 24, 1772, since the first dated entry (p. 6) is Saturday, October 31, 1772. From this last date, the extracts are arranged in chronological order for every Saturday (occasionally every other Saturday) through Saturday, September 4, 1773. The original item probably carries the extracts through to the end of September 1773 which would be a full, or almost a full, year—suggesting that the volume was published in late 1773 or, possibly, 1774.

The volume seems to have been published in Barbados and compiled by John Orderson. Its printing style and various other physical features indicate a colonial imprint; moreover, this is a very rare item and the rarest Barbados published materials were printed on the island in the eighteenth and early nineteenth centuries. Orderson published the *Barbados Mercury* during this period. Starting around 1771, he was a partner in the printery that published the newspaper but with his partner's death on October 3, 1772, he carried on the business alone (E. M. Shilstone, "Some Notes on Early

Printing Presses and Newspapers in Barbados," *JBMHS*, 26, 1958, 27-31). Orderson may have published this volume to commemorate his first year as sole editor of the *Mercury*. He continued to publish and edit the paper until at least the early 1780s when one of his sons also became involved.

The only known copy of this volume is the one described here; its value is enhanced because there are no known copies of the *Barbados Mercury* for the period it covers.

WESLEY, JOHN
Thoughts upon slavery.
London, 1774. *53 pp.* [JCB]
This indictment of slavery and the slave trade by the celebrated Methodist occasionally mentions Barbados.

DALRYMPLE, ALEXANDER
A collection of voyages chiefly in the southern Atlantic Ocean. Published from original m.s.s.
London, 1775. [JCB]
Each voyage has its own title page and pagination, and is mainly in the format of ship's logs. "Dr. Halley's first voyage" (pp. 13-15, 16, 21) mentions a short visit to Barbados in 1699, presents navigational data, and observes how scarce wood is on the island. In "A journal of a voyage made . . . in His Majesty's ship Paramore Pink," Halley records navigational data and mentions a yellow fever epidemic during his three-day visit to Barbados in 1700 (pp. 61-62).

SENHOUSE, JOSEPH
Senhouse papers: The diary of Joseph Senhouse [1776-1778].
See below, Senhouse 1985-1988.

[QUIER, J.] (ED.)
Letters and essays on the small-pox and innoculation, the measles . . . of the West Indies.
London, 1778. *320 pp.* [JCB]
Authored by various medical doctors with firsthand knowledge of the West Indies, the articles deal with several human, and some cattle, diseases. Although largely treating Jamaica, and to a lesser degree Antigua and Martinique, Barbados is briefly mentioned (pp. 203-10, 219) in a general discussion of yellow fever. In 1735, the author, a British naval doctor, visited

the island; the healthy 250-man crew on board the warship was soon stricken by yellow fever. There is a detailed account of a couple of the patients, and the unsuccessful treatment to save their lives.

RUSSELL, WILLIAM
The history of America, from its discovery by Columbus to the conclusion of the late war.
London, 1778. 2 vols.   [NYPL]
Based on secondary sources, the section on Barbados (vol. 2, pp. 74-76), reviews the island's political and economic history, discusses its present political and trade position, including its place in the slave trade, and makes a few comments on Bridgetown.

VERDUN DE LA CRENNE
Voyage fait par ordre du roi en 1771 et 1772, en diverse parties de l'Europe, de l'Afrique et de l'Amerique.
Paris, 1778. *500 pp.*   [JCB]
Volume 2 (pp. 122-24) discusses the longtitude and latitude of Barbados, and attempts to reconcile discrepancies between various eighteenth-century discussions and maps.

WEST INDIA merchant. Being a series of papers originally printed under that signature in the London Evening Post.
London, 1778. *206 pp.*   [JCB]
Authored by an English merchant with commercial interests in the West Indies, the "papers" treat trade problems between Britain and its American colonies, particularly between the Continental colonies and the West Indies as this trade was affected by the American Revolution. A "paper" of June 6, 1776 (pp. 115-24) reproduces an address from the Barbados Assembly to the British Crown; it discusses how the disruption of trade with the Continental colonies is adversely affecting the island's economy and the supply of foodstuffs for slaves.

JEFFERYS, THOMAS
The West-Indian atlas; or a general description of the West Indies.
London, 1780.   [NL]
An alternate title: *The West-India atlas: or, a compendious description of the West-Indies.* Published after the death of Jefferys, the author of the introduction notes that "this work unites [Jefferys'] *Atlas* [London, 1775; see JSH-71] and *Pilot* [*A complete pilot*

for the West Indies . . . done from actual surveys, London—a collection of about 27 maps with two pages of text], shewing both the geographic and hydrographic parts." Page 20 contains a lengthy description of Barbados, focusing on its physical geography but also giving an overview of its political and administrative organization, trade, and towns; the last date mentioned is 1770. The *Atlas* includes a full page detailed map of Barbados, "surveyed by William Mayo, engraved and improved by Thomas Jefferys," London, February 20, 1775.

RODNEY, GEORGE
News from Admiral Rodney. Extract of a letter from Admiral Rodney to Mr.Stephens, dated in Carlisle Bay Barbadoes, May 31, 1780.
[London? 1780]. *Broadside.*   [CL]
In this apparently rare item, Rodney briefly reports the provisioning of his fleet at St. Lucia and describes naval encounters with a French fleet near Martinique. He records his return to Barbados "in order to put the sick and wounded on shore, and repair the squadron"; sixty-eight men were killed and close to three hundred wounded.

MARKHAM, ROBERT
Sympathy in distress, recommended in a sermon, occasioned by the heavy sufferings of our fellow-subjects in the West-India islands, and preached in the parish church of St. Mary, Whitechapel.
London, 1781. *15 pp.*   [JCB]
Directed toward soliciting contributions for the "present extraordinary and intolerable sufferings of the inhabitants of Barbadoes, St. Vincent's, St. Lucia . . . and other places lately visited by tempests . . . ." Barbados, in particular, was severely affected by a hurricane in 1780.

[ESTWICK, SAMUEL]
Considerations on the present decline of the sugar-trade; and on the means which are proposed, by the refiners of London, for reinstating it.
[London], 1782. *58 pp.*   [JCB]
Listed in JSH-71, but not consulted. The author's name is not published, but the JCB copy's title page contains a contemporary manuscript notation "written by Saml. Estwick Esq. Agent for Barbadoes & Secy. to Chelsea Hospital." Arguing for the protection of British West Indian sugar interests and sugar growers, this item

provides some sugar trade statistics and discusses the business of sugar refining in Britain, the politics of the sugar trade, sugar duties, competition between French and British produced sugar, and the illicit trade in sugar.

GREAT BRITAIN, LORDS COMMISSION-ERS OF APPEALS IN PRIZE CAUSES
Before the . . . lords commissioners of appeals in prize causes. Appeal from the vice-admiralty court of Barbadoes. De Jonge Jan & Theodore, Jan Reygers, master.
[London, 1782].   [JCB]
Bound into a volume (given the binder's title *Prize Cases in Admiralty Courts: North America and West Indies, 1780-1782*) with many other similar cases from different courts in North America and the West Indies. The dates of hearings are inscribed in manuscript. Concerns a Dutch cargo vessel, bound from Suriname to Amsterdam, that was taken by a British naval vessel and brought to Barbados. Contains the appellant's and respondent's cases as well as an appendix with depositions of various eyewitnesses (pp. 324-33). The *ESTC* also locates a copy in the BL.

*GREAT BRITAIN, LORDS COMMIS-SIONERS OF APPEALS IN PRIZE CAUSES
Before the . . . lords commissioners of appeals in prize causes. Commerce, Gerrit Zowe, master . . . An appeal from the vice-admiralty court . . . of Barbadoes.
[London, 1782].   [BL]
Two items: The appellant's case and the appendix to the respondent's case. Citation and location from the *ESTC.*

HUNT, ISAAC
A discourse delivered at St. Paul's church, Shadwell, for the benefit of the West-India sufferers of the islands of Jamaica and Barbados.
London, 1782. *34 pp.*   [JCB]
Delivered by the Barbadian-born Reverend Hunt, the "discourse" refers to relief for victims of Barbados's devastating 1780 hurricane. Mentioned in JSH-71, but not consulted.

ANDERSON, ALEXANDER
[Geography and History of St.Vincent, 1783 or 1784].
See below, Anderson 1983.

*GREAT BRITAIN, LORDS COMMIS-SIONERS OF APPEALS IN PRIZE CAUSES
Before the . . . lords commissioners of appeals in prize causes. De Maastrom, Christian Eeg, master . . . . An appeal from the vice-admiralty court . . . of Barbadoes.
[London, 1783].   [BL]
Two items: the appellant's case and its appendix. Citation and location from the *ESTC*; a copy of the appendix is also held by the Pierpont Morgan Library, New York City.

*GREAT BRITAIN, LORDS COMMIS-SIONERS OF APPEALS IN PRIZE CAUSES
Before the . . . lords commissioners of appeals in prize causes. De Jonge William & Jacob, Hendrick Kavinga, master . . . . An appeal from the vice-admiralty court . . . of Barbadoes.
[London, 1783].   [BL]
The appellant's case. Citation and location from the *ESTC.*

NATIVE OF THE WEST INDIES
Poems on subjects arising in England, and the West Indies.
London, 1783. *108 pp.*   [BL]
Internal evidence suggests the author was most familiar with Antigua and Nevis, although the few poems (and their accompanying explanatory notes which sometimes provide information on social customs) that deal with the West Indies usually do not specify particular islands. One of the short poems, "A True Story" (pp. 83-84) is set in Barbados and tells about two male slaves in love with the same woman who cannot choose between them; one night all three commit suicide "and seek their much-lov'd country in the grave."

SHEFFIELD, JOHN
Observations on the commerce of the American states.
London, 1783. 2nd ed. *122 pp.*   [JCB]
Detailed discussion of trade issues. Although focusing on the U.S. and Britain, there are frequent references to the British West Indies in general with occasional specific references to Barbados. Discussions are organized around the main types of import and exports between England, the U.S., and the West Indies, and between the U.S. and the West Indies, such as, woolens, cutlery, "porcelein and earthen ware," glass, shoes, buttons, books, hats,

haberdashery, paints, cordage, medicines, paper, silks, lumber, spermaceti candles, sugar, rum, molasses, horses, wheat, and salt fish. This type of organization provides a systematic perspective on the types of material goods and the uses to which they were put in the U.S. and the West Indies. The Appendix has a number of statistical tables on various trade matters and particular territories. Barbados is listed in tables which detail the quantity of various agricultural products imported into Britain in 1772 and 1773 (tables 5 and 6), exported from Scotland in 1772 (table 8), and the monetary value of all goods imported to and exported from England in the early 1770s (table 18). The 6th edition (London, 1784 [JCB]) also contains tabular materials on Barbados.

COPY OF a letter from a gentleman in Barbados to his friend in Glasgow. A full true and particular account of a most dreadful earthquake, which happened at the island of Barbados . . . on 16th of December 1784. Glasgow [1784]. *Broadside.*
Catalog no. 1033 (London, 1983) of the London bookseller Bernard Quaritch notes that "the earthquake provided 'a scene affecting and terrible beyond description' . . . . This is an excellent letter, full of news." Whatever news this item contains, there is no corroborative evidence that an earthquake occurred in Barbados in 1784—certainly nothing on the scale suggested by the catalog notation.

*ELLIS AND PERCH
Cursory observations on the last debates of the assembly.
Barbados, 1784.
Cited by authors' last names and title in Karl Watson, *The Civilized Island, Barbados, a Social History, 1750-1816* (Ph.D. diss., Gainesville, University of Florida, 1975, p. 230). Watson saw this item advertised in the *Barbados Mercury* newspaper but had not personally seen it and was unaware of any copy (personal communication). Years of search have failed to locate a copy.

*GREAT BRITAIN, LORDS COMMIS-SIONERS OF APPEALS IN PRIZE CAUSES
Before the . . . lords commissioners of appeals in prize causes. De Noord Steeren, Herman Samsing, master. An appeal from the vice-admiralty court . . . of Barbadoes.
[London, 1784].   [BL]

Three items: the respondent's case; translation of letters contained in the process transmitted from Barbadoes, on behalf of the claimant; the appellant's case. Citation and location from the *ESTC.*

*GREAT BRITAIN, LORDS COMMIS-SIONERS OF APPEALS IN PRIZE CAUSES
Before the . . . lords commissioners of appeals in prize causes. Het Huys Brandenburg, Frans de Clerck, master . . . . An appeal from the vice-admiralty court of Barbadoes.
[London, 1784].   [BL]
The appellant's case. Citation and location from the *ESTC.*

[BOUCHER, FRANCIS]
A dissertation on the revolutions of states, and empires, with some considerations on the blessings of peace, and the evils of war.
Barbados, 1785. 22 pp.   [BOA].
Dedicated to Barbados's Governor David Parry, printed by the Barbadian printer John Edward Orderson, and including many prominent Barbadians in its "list of subscribers," this pamphlet generally treats, from a theological perspective, the themes indicated in the title; more specifically, it addresses issues raised by the American Revolution. Boucher calls for acceptance of the fact of American independence, as "humiliating as such a concession may be to . . . an enterprizing monarch, and [as] degrading . . . [it is to] the grandeur, and lessening the power of a great empire." Reconciliation to American independence can be achieved when it is recognized that it results from "the powerful workings of Providence." In general, war is "the severest evil and heaviest affliction that can befall a people," and peace brings a variety of advantages, including, for Barbadians in particular, the "pleasing prospects of an uninterrupted navigation and extensive commerce, whereby we may be supplied . . . with the necessaries . . . [and] conveniencies of life."
    The only known copy of this pamphlet is in the BOA. In his *Catalogue of the Washington collection in the Boston Athenaeum* (Boston, 1897, pp. 29-30), Appelton Griffin writes that the pamphlet had been sent to George Washington by John Tucker of Barbados, at the request of the author, who Tucker describes as a "worthy clergyman of this island." Griffin identifies the author and reproduces a letter written by Boucher to Tucker on June 6, 1785. In this letter

Boucher says that a more appropriate title for his work would be "A discourse on the cessation of hostilities, & the establishment of the Independence of America"; in the "course of his studies," Boucher wrote, he was led to the conclusion that the "establishment of the independence of America [was] an extraordinary dispensation of Providence."

[CHETWOOD, WILLIAM]
The voyages, dangerous adventures and imminent escapes of Captain Richard Falconer . . . intermixed with the voyages and adventures of Thomas Randal.
Manchester, 1785. *379 pp.* [JCB]
Although the epistle dedicatory inscription is signed by Richard Falconer as the author, the JCB catalog identifies this as the pseudonym for William Chetwood. The book describes a 1699 voyage from England. The first port of call is Barbados where approximately two weeks are spent in this "richest and best peopled island in all America." Only a few comments are offered (pp. 21-22) on the island's geography, harbors, and towns; the reader is referred to Ligon for more details (JSH-71, p. 4).

*GREAT BRITAIN, LORDS COMMISSIONERS OF APPEALS IN PRIZE CAUSES
Before the . . . lords commissioners of appeals in prize causes. De Jonge Jan en Theodore, Jan Reygers, master . . . . On an appeal from the vice-admiralty court . . . of Barbados.
[London, 1785]. [BL]
The appellant's case. Citation and location from the *ESTC.*

*GREAT BRITAIN, LORDS COMMISSIONERS OF APPEALS IN PRIZE CAUSES
Before the . . . lords commissioners of appeals in prize causes. An appeal from the vice-admiralty court . . . of Barbados. Bella Guidita, Giovanni Lalli, master.
[London, 1785]. [BL]
Three items: the appendix to the respondent's case; the case on behalf of the captor and respondent; the appellants' and interveners' case. Citation and location from the *ESTC.*

*GREAT BRITAIN, LORDS COMMISSIONERS OF APPEALS IN PRIZE CAUSES
Before the . . . lords commissioners of appeals in prize causes. Noord Stiernen, Herman Samsing, master . . . . on appeal from

Barbadoes. *The appellant's case, on further proof as to the property of the ship.*
[London, 1785]. [BL]
Citation and location from the *ESTC.*

*GREAT BRITAIN, LORDS COMMISSIONERS OF APPEALS IN PRIZE CAUSES
Before the . . . lords commissioners of appeals in prize causes. Appeal from the vice-admiralty court of . . . Barbadoes. The Arend of Zee, Jan Hendrick Stebbes, master.
[London, 1785]. [BL]
Three items: the respondent's case, its appendix, and the appellant's case. Citation and location from the *ESTC.*

*GREAT BRITAIN, LORDS COMMISSIONERS OF APPEALS IN PRIZE CAUSES
Before the . . . lords commissioners of appeals in prize causes. The America, Charlesvan Weysmantel, master. Appeal from the vice-Admiralty court of . . . Barbadoes.
[London, 1785]. [BL]
Four items: the respondent's case and appendix, and the appellant's case and appendix. Citation and location from the *ESTC.*

*GREAT BRITAIN, LORDS COMMISSIONERS OF APPEALS IN PRIZE CAUSES
Before the . . . lords commissioners of appeals in prize causes. Le Count de Colloredo, Philip Francois Macquet, master. Appeal from the vice-Admiralty court in Barbadoes.
[London, 1785]. [BL]
Six items: respondent's and appellant's cases and their appendixes; "further proofs as to the uses and quality of the cargo, on behalf of the captors and respondents"; "further case on behalf of the claimant and appellant." Citation and location from the *ESTC.*

[TOBIN, JAMES]
Cursory remarks upon the reverend Mr. Ramsay's essay on the treatment and conversion of African slaves in the sugar colonies.
London, 1785. *168 pp.* [JCB]
The author resided in the West Indies for "several years"; he is identified in the JCB copy. Focusing on slavery in the British islands, this detailed and systematic rebuttal to James Ramsay's celebrated work (JSH-71, p. 47) occasionally mentions Barbados, "the most declining island in our possession."

A FORM of prayer to be used on the tenth of October.
Bridgetown, 1786. *11 pp.*   [JCB]
Simply a prayer for Anglican use. The October date was set aside to commemorate deliverance from the 1780 hurricane. Rare.

ASSOCIATES OF DOCTOR THOMAS BRAY FOR FOUNDING CLERICAL LIBRARIES AND SUPPORTING NEGRO SCHOOLS

Abstract of the proceedings of the Associates of Doctor Bray, for the year 1785.
[London, 1786]. *20 pp.*   [JCB]
Under the title "Negro Schools. Barbadoes," pp. 7-14 of this item include a "letter" from William Duke, rector of St. Thomas. With funds provided by the Associates for about twenty-five "young learners," Duke intends to shortly "institute a proper school" in his parish "to teach Negro children to read" so that they can be "trained in the faith and fear of God"; he has notified his (white) parishioners of his intentions. The "letter" outlines Duke's criteria for accepting pupils, describes mechanical problems he anticipates in establishing the school, and details how he plans to preach to slaves and organize services for them. In a major portion of the "letter," Duke explains to his parishioners why he is interested in preaching to slaves, and argues that "the principles of Christianity, . . . and the inculcating of the duties of fidelity and obedience to their respective owners, is a work worthy of attempt." His sermons will stress such topics as why "fidelity and obedience to their owners" is necessary, how they "ought to behave to their superiors," and that "destroying life by poison, or any secret means" is "cruel and unlawful"; also, "an exhortation against polygamy and unlawful concubinage," an examination and refutation of "superstitious notions concerning their dead, their funeral rites, and commemoration of their dead family," and that "witchcraft, obeah, conjurers, oaths or swearing upon grave dirt [will be] shewn to be foolish and absurd." Duke hopes his sermons will cause slaves to reject "some pernicious principles and tenets . . . that make them so much the dupes of superstition, and often destroy that interest their . . . owners have in their labour and service." In all, the sermons were to depreciate a variety of important beliefs and behaviors of African derivation, as well as encourage conformity and compliance to the slave regime—common themes in the Christianization of slaves.

The son of William Duke, a former clerk of the Barbados House of Assembly, the Barbadian-born Reverend William Duke was himself a plantation owner and, undoubtedly, a slave owner. From 1758 until his death in October 1786 he was the Rector of St. Thomas; he also sometimes served as a Justice of the Peace and from 1776 until his death he was Chaplain to the House of Assembly (see *JBMHS*, 14, 1947, 106, 186; 15, 1947, 64; 16, 1948, 33, 72, 73). Duke's effort to establish a "charity school" for slaves may have been the earliest such attempt in Barbados, and was one of the earliest stated intentions by a parochial minister to have at least some slaves in his parish instructed in reading. It is not certain, however, if the school was ever established. Duke died not long after his "letter" was published, and in 1788 the Bishop of London was notified that "the zeal and industry of the late Mr. Duke, though high commendable, have left no visible traces of the efficacy of his labours" (Clergy of Barbados to Bishop Porteus, September 26, 1788; Fulham Papers, vol. 16, pp. 174-75, Lambeth Palace Library, London).

SMITH, JOHN S.

A letter from Capt. J. S. Smith to the Revd. Mr. Hill on the state of the Negroe slaves.
London, 1786. *51 pp.*   [JCB]
Although this is cataloged (following *Anglo-American Cataloging Rules*, 2nd ed.) under the authorship of Smith, actually it was written by the celebrated abolitionist, James Ramsay. The tract is signed and dated at the end, "James Ramsay, Tefton [England], Feb. 20, 1786," and he has written most of its pages; as the "editor" identified on the title page he brings Smith's letter into print.

Smith's eight-page letter vindicates Ramsay's views about "the ill treatment of slaves" in the West Indies where, as a naval officer, he had been stationed in the 1770s; he sometimes refers to specific islands, for example, Antigua, Grenada, which he knew from first hand experience. The bulk of this item, however, is Ramsay's discussion of reactions to his *Essay on the treatment and conversion of African slaves in the British sugar colonies* (London, 1784; see

JSH-71), an elaboration on the "wretched condition" and "ill treatment" of British West Indian slaves, and a discussion of "Free Negroes" and wage work on sugar plantations; work in sugar could also be performed, he argues, by free white laborers because "ever since the first settlement of the sugar colonies, white people have been accustomed there to much harder labour than the common plantation work." Barbados is cited as a case in point.

FRANCKLYN, GILBERT

Observations, occasioned by the attempts made in England to effect the abolition of the slave trade; shewing, the manner in which Negroes are treated in the British colonies in the West-Indies.

Kingston, Jamaica, 1788. *97 pp.*   [LC] Francklyn claims considerable personal experience in the West Indies and was in Barbados "sometime about the year 1780." He feels particularly qualified to address the reality of slave treatment, but LJR (p. 504) notes, he was really "a member of the West India group in London" and a propagandist for its interests. *Observations* strongly defends the slave trade, argues for Biblical justification of slavery and that West Indian slaves are well-treated, and "their lot is to be envied by the generality of the peasants in every part of Europe"— common themes in the proslavery literature. Pages 48-61 specifically deal with Barbados and various issues relating to the treatment of slaves and their material welfare; these pages are intended to specifically refute (as indeed is much of Francklyn's work) the Barbadian-born Reverend Robert Boucher Nicholls's criticism of slave treatment in the West Indies (see JSH-71, p. 51). *Observations* was reprinted in London in 1789 [BL, LC, JCB].

[LEIGH, WILLIAM]

Remarks on the slave trade, and the slavery of the Negroes.

London, 1788. *66 pp.*   [JCB] The author's name is inscribed in contemporary manuscript on the title page of the JCB copy. An abolitionist pamphlet, not based on the author's firsthand experiences. Barbados is briefly discussed (p. 66), but the information derives from Ramsay (London, 1784; see JSH-71, p. 47).

LIND, JAMES

An essay on diseases incidental to Europeans in hot climates.

London, 1788. 4th ed. *357 pp.*   [JCB] Contains several comments on how healthy Barbados's climate is for Europeans (pp. 113, 201, 210-11); the author gives no indication that he ever visited the island.

GREAT BRITAIN, HOUSE OF COMMONS

Minutes of the evidence taken (in the last session of parliament) before the committee of the whole house, to whom the bill for providing certain temporary regulations respecting the transportation of the natives of Africa, in British ships, to the West Indies, and elsewhere, was committed.

[London], 1789. *58 pp.*   [JCB] One of a number of similar items (see, for example, JSH-71, pp. 106-7) relating to hearings by the House of Commons on the issue of the slave trade. Involves transcriptions of testimonies given by slaving captains and senior crew members, and provides detailed information on the nature of the trade, particularly the middle passage. Barbados is briefly mentioned in several places in the testimony of Robert Norris.

[STEELE, JOSHUA]

To the equity and policy of a great nation. Barbados, August 10. From a real colonist.

[Barbados, 1789]. *Broadsheet.*   [LC, NL] Described in JSH-71, but authorship was uncertain although Steele was suggested; William Dickson (1814, p. 20) establishes Steele's authorship with certainty.

DUKE, WILLIAM

A course of plain and familiar lectures on the Christian covenant, on the articles of the Christian faith, and on . . . baptism and the Lord's supper. Chiefly delivered in the parish-church of St. Thomas, in the island of Barbadoes.

Gloucester, 1790. 2nd ed. *141 pp.*   [BL] Reverend Duke had been rector of St. Thomas. Clearly intended only for white congregations, his sermons contain no references to secular matters. This edition was published four years after Duke's death in 1786; it is unknown where and when the first edition was published. The *NUC* lists 1794 and 1811 London editions at LCP and CL, respectively.

*GREAT BRITAIN, PARLIAMENT, HOUSE OF COMMONS
[Proceedings. 1790]. Reports from the Committee of Engineers, on the probable expence of fortifications in the islands of Grenada, Barbadoes, St. Vincent's, Dominica, Antigua, and St. Christopher's.
[London, 1790].   [BL, NYPL]
Citation and locations from the ESTC.

*PARRY, DAVID
A proclamation.
[Barbados?] 1791.
Issued by the governor of Barbados, who "caused [the proclamation] to be published"; relates to "the scandlous and shameful practice of debasing the current coin of this island." With related documents, reprinted in Pridmore (1965, pp. 296-298; see below); a similar proclamation may have been published a few days later (JBMHS, 21, 1954, 20-22).

MILNE, J.
Method of planting cotton in Demerary and Surinam [and] Method of planting cotton in Barbados.
London, 1792. 4 pp.   [JCB]
Apparently rare and based on the author's personal experiences, the Barbados section (pp. 2-4) very briefly describes how cotton should be planted and then discusses its economic advantages.

FRANKLIN, BENJAMIN
Works of the late Doctor Benjamin Franklin: consisting of his life written by himself.
London [1793]. 2 vols.   [JCB]
Included in JSH-71, but not consulted. In his youth Franklin worked for Samuel Keimer, an early printer in Barbados. Volume 1 (pp. 67-182, passim) contains quite a few references to Keimer, his life and work as a printer in Philadelphia until creditors forced him to sell out: "he betook himself to Barbadoes, where he lived for some time in a very impoverished state" (p. 180). Keimer's apprentice, David Harry, bought the business from Keimer and eventually went to Barbadoes, established a printery there, and employed "his old master as journeyman." They did not get along and Harry got into debt; he sold his press and types and returned to Pennsylvania while the person who purchased Harry's equipment employed Keimer "to manage the business, but he

died a few years later" (pp. 181-82). Pages 140-82, passim, contain occasional information on David Harry.

*[SCOTT, GENERAL W. A.]
The rules of Whist. Being a compendium of easy rules . . . with maxims.
Bridgetown, 1796. 4th ed. 26 pp.   [LCP]
Published by Matthew Carbery, the LCP's copy (acquired in 1971) is the only one known; no information is available about earlier editions, nor are any copies known. The LCP Annual Report for 1971 (Philadelphia, 1972, p. 23), notes that the LCP has failed "to find anything helpful" concerning the work or its author; moreover, the Report expresses scepticism over the Library of Congress identification of the author (based on its copy of the 10th edition [London, 1815]) as "Lieutenant-General W. A. Scott." I have been unable to find any information that would elucidate authorship.

WINTERBOTHAM, WILLIAM
An historical, geographical, commercial, and philosophical view of the United States of America, and of the European settlements in America and the West Indies.
New York, 1796. 4 vols.   [LC]
Brief descriptions (vol. 4, pp. 242-47) of Barbados's geography, climate, flora and fauna, history of settlement, population, governmental structure, and so forth. Information appears to be taken from standard published sources.

MORSE, JEDIDIAH
The American gazetteer. A . . . full and accurate account of the American continent, also of the West-India islands.
Boston, 1797. 619 pp.   [LC]
Entries are arranged alphabetically. In a little more than two columns the Barbados entry covers conventional topics, such as, location, geography, population, history— all apparently drawn from standard published sources; also separate brief entries on Bridgetown, Speightstown, and Oistin which contain some factual errors.

BERNKOPF, FRIEDERICH ANTON
Friedrich Anton Bernkopf eines Badersohns aus Gratz gefahrvolle seereise nach Ostindien.
Gratz, 1798. 120 pp.   [JCB]
According to the JCB catalog this is an "apparently" fictional work whose author

identifies himself as the son of a barber from Gratz, Austria. This item, dealing with the West Indies, is a narrative of adventures at sea. Barbados is briefly mentioned with respect to naval battles offshore, landing at Bridgetown to replenish supplies, and the description of a sword-fish (pp. 43, 47-49).

*GREAT BRITAIN, LORDS COMMISSIONERS OF APPEALS IN PRIZE CAUSES
Before the . . . lords commissioners of appeals in prize causes. Barbadoes in Admiralty. (An appeal from the vice-admiralty court of . . . Barbadoes.) John Salisbury, . . . of his Majesty's ship Beaulieu, against the sloop Ranger, Ebenezer Gove, master.
[London, 1798].   [BL]
Four items: the appellant's case and appendix; the respondent's case and appendix; Citation and location from the *ESTC.*

*GREAT BRITAIN, LORDS COMMISSIONERS OF APPEALS IN PRIZE CAUSES
Before the . . . lords commissioners of appeals in prize causes. (An appeal from the vice-admiralty court of . . . Barbadoes.) The schooner Swan, Benjamin Hawkes.
[London, 1798].   [BM]
The appellant's case. Citation and location from the *ESTC.*

*GREAT BRITAIN, LORDS COMMISSIONERS OF APPEALS IN PRIZE CAUSES
Before the . . . lords commissioners of appeals in prize causes. (An appeal from the vice-admiralty court . . . of Barbadoes.) The Resolution, John Burlingham, master.
[London, 1798].   [BL]
The appellant's case. Citation and location from the *ESTC.*

*GREAT BRITAIN, LORDS COMMISSIONERS OF APPEALS IN PRIZE CAUSES
Before the . . . lords commissioners of appeals in prize causes. The Lady Washington, Ephraim Lombard, master. An appeal from the vice-admiralty court of Barbadoes.
[London, 1798].   [BL]
Three items: the appendix, the respondent's and appellant's case. Citation and location from the *ESTC .*

*GREAT BRITAIN, LORDS COMMISSIONERS OF APPEALS IN PRIZE CAUSES
Before the . . . lords commissioners of appeals in prize causes. The ship America, Tristram

Gardner, master. An appeal from the vice-admiralty court of Barbadoes.
[London, 1798].   [BL]
Three items: the appendix, and cases for the appellant and respondent. Citation and location from the *ESTC.*

THORNHILL, HENRY
A narrative of the insurrection and rebellion in the island of Grenada.
Barbados, 1798. *63 pp.*   [BL, JCB]
The author witnessed the 1795 events he describes, and unsuccessfully tried to get this item published in Grenada. After arriving in Barbados in January 1797, he found a newly established printer, Gilbert Ripnel, "in the Bay, between the two Bridges," who agreed to publication.

JORDAN, GIBBES WALKER
An account of the Irides or Coronae which appear around, and contiguous to, the bodies of the sun, moon, and other luminous objects.
London, 1799. *46 pp.*   [BL]
One of several scientific works by the same author (see below, Walker 1799, 1800, 1820), none of which deal with Barbados per se. Jordan was a Barbadian who became the island's agent in London and served in that capacity from 1800 until his death in 1823 (see *JBMHS*, 1, 1933, 66; 16, 1949, 148; 20, 1952, 12; RS, pp. 368, 415-16). For Jordan's other publications on a variety of social, political, and economic topics, see JSH-71, passim.

JORDAN, GIBBES WALKER
The observations of Newton concerning the inflections of light; accompanied by other observations differing from his; and appearing to lead to a change of his theory of light and colours.
London, 1799. *134 pp.*   [NYPL]
See Jordan 1799 (*Account of the Irides*).

*GREAT BRITAIN, LORDS COMMISSIONERS OF APPEALS IN PRIZE CAUSES
Before the . . . lords commissioners of appeals in prize causes. (An appeal from Barbadoes.) The schooner Hope, Daniel Farley master.
London [1800].   [BL]
Two items: the appendix and the appellant's case. Citation and location from the *ESTC.*

*GREAT BRITAIN, LORDS COMMIS-
SIONERS OF APPEALS IN PRIZE CAUSES

*Before the . . . the lords commissioners of
appeals in prize causes. The Hope, otherwise
L'Esperance, Obed Paddock, master. An
appeal from the vice-Admiralty Court of
Barbadoes. Case and appendix for the further
hearing.*

London [1800?].   [BL]

Citation and location from the *ESTC.*

JORDAN, GIBBES WALKER

*New observations concerning the colours of
thin transparent bodies, shewing those phae-
nomena to be inflections of light, and that the
Newtonian fits of easy transmission and
reflection derived from them have no existence.*

London, 1800. *106 pp.* [BL, NYPL, LCP]

See Jordan 1799 (*Account of the Irides*).

1801-1988

*[CLINTON, J.]

[Plantation management in Barbados.]

[London, ca. 1800.]

A book attributed to the above author, with
a constructed title and evidence for its
existence is discussed in JSH-71. No trace
of this book has been found, but additional
evidence that it was published is found in a
list of books relating to Barbados that was
compiled by an early nineteenth-century
Barbadian; he refers to "Management of
Estates by Clinton" (*JBMHS*, 21, 1953, 21).

CLARK, THOMAS

*Observations on the nature and cure of fevers,
and of diseases of the West and East Indies,
and of America.*

Edinburgh and London, 1801. *257 pp.*
                                    [SIU]

As a British Army surgeon, Clark spent
approximately seven months in Barbados
over the period 1793-94. Pages 98-117
directly or indirectly relate to his
experiences in the West Indies, primarily
Barbados, and are mainly concerned with
the medical problems, principally yellow
fever, he encountered among the British
troops. Virtually no nonmedical
observations are offered, but occasional
brief information is given on matters
pertaining to the military forces stationed
at Barbados.

*ORDERSON, J. W.

Orderson's colonial register for . . . Barbados.

Bridgetown [1802].

Listed in JSH-71 under the title *Colonial
Register for 1802 . . .* , but not located. The

NSTC locates a copy of this very rare item
at O-BO.

BROUGHAM, HENRY

*An inquiry into the colonial policy of the
European powers.*

Edinburgh, 1803. 2 vols.   [JCB]

Several references to Barbados in a
discussion of the negative consequences of
the four-and-one-half percent duty on
exports, first passed in the seventeenth
century, and its implications for
maintaining the colonial establishment
(vol. 1, pp. 550-55).

NORMAN, WILLIAM

The new improved West-India pilot.

Boston, 1803.   [JCB]

Eleven nautical maps and ten pages of
descriptive "sailing directions." Two
paragraphs on Barbados (p. 2) describe
approaches to the island, mention shore
points from which to get bearings, and
note precautionary measures to be taken
along various coastal areas.

*ECCENTRIC BIOGRAPHY; or, memoirs of
remarkable female characters, ancient and
modern.*

Worcester, Mass., 1804. *338 pp.*   [H]

The first American edition (an earlier
edition was published in London in 1803),
containing brief biographical sketches of
about 100 women, including Joan of Arc,
Catherine the Great, and so forth. The first
sketch (pp. 9-11) deals with Alice, "a
female slave, and native of America . . .
born in Philadelphia, of parents who came
from Barbadoes"; nothing is said of her

parents or Barbados. Alice was known for her piety and vivid memory of Philadelphia's early history; she died in that city in 1802, at the age of 116. The frontspiece is an engraving of Alice in old age.

M'CALLUM, PIERRE F.
Travels in Trinidad during the months of February, March and April 1803.
Liverpool, 1805. *352 pp.*   [JCB, LC, BL]
The author spent one day in Barbados, apparently all of it in Bridgetown. He briefly comments (pp. 10-12) on Barbados's history and Governor Seaforth, and notes that Bridgetown "has an antique appearance; but what strikes the stranger's attention is the number of old women, cats, and parrots." The Barbadian, he observes, "will not allow the island to be in the West Indies, much less that he is either a Crab (Caribbee) or Creole, but a true Barbadian," and that Barbadians are "said to be both friendly and hospitable to strangers," something his limited experience confirms.

*REDDISH, S.
A digest of the laws of the customs, as they relate to the plantations, carefully compiled from the statutes at large.
[Barbados? 1805?]
An advertisement in the *Barbados Mercury and Bridgetown Gazette* of 5 March 1805 notes that the author is "Comptroller of His Majesty's Customs at the Port of Bridgetown" and that his work is "preparing for the press and will be published in August next"; a prospectus is also given. Efforts to locate a copy of this item or to verify its existence have failed; it may never have been actually published.

GREGOIRE, HENRI B.
De la littérature des Nègres.
Paris, 1808. *287 pp.*   [BL]
Contains a brief biographical sketch of the "good and religious Joseph Rachel, a free Negro of Barbadoes" (p. 124), based entirely on Dickson 1789 (see JSH-71, pp. 52-53).

ORIGINAL ACCOUNT of the desperate engagement and capture of the General Washington, Alexander Boyle, commander.
London [1808]. *28 pp.*   [JCB]
Pages 24-28 include the separately titled *Dreadful effects of a hurricane, which happened*

at Barbadoes in 1780, by which a number of souls, whites and blacks were destroyed, and several buildings were demolished; with preliminary observations, communicated by an officer of His Majesty's ship Quebec. This is a superficial account of one of the most devastating storms in Barbados's history; the publication date is given on p. 26.

SEAFORTH, FRANCIS M.
"An account of some new species of Piper with a few current observations on the genus. By Mr. John Vaughan Thompson. Communicated by the Right Honourable Lord Seaforth."
The Transactions of the Linnean Society of London, vol. 9, 1808, *pp. 200-203.*
The Governor of Barbados notes that his original interest was the study of different varieties of this botanical genus but "professional occupations prevented me from carrying this intention into execution so completely." Read before the society in 1807, this paper technically describes plant varieties in Trinidad, St. Vincent, and Grenada; there is no mention of Barbados. For more on Governor Seaforth and his contributions to botany, see R. A. Howard, "Early botanical records from the West Indies, particularly Barbados" (*Botanical Journal of the Linnean Society* 79, 1979, 65-96).

DERROTERO DE las islas Antillas, de las costas de tierra firme.
Madrid, 1810. *455 pp.*   [JCB]
Instructions to sailors. The Barbados section (pp. 68-69) describes approaches to the island, geographical features to be aware of, how to anchor in Carlisle Bay and the precautions that should be taken in so doing.

DICKSON, WILLIAM
(To be shortly published, if encouraged by an adequate subscription.) A plan for the mitigation of slavery.
Edinburgh, 1810. *Broadsheet.* [JCB, LCP]
In this rare item, Dickson attempts to raise subscribers for his book *Mitigation of Slavery* (see below, Dickson 1814).

DUNCAN, ARCHIBALD (Ed.)
The mariner's chronicle; or, authentic and complete history of popular shipwrecks.
London, 1810. Vol. 1. *334 pp.*   [BL]
Contains two narratives relating to Barbados; the editor does not give his

sources for these narratives. "The sufferings of part of the crew of the ship Thomas, of Liverpool, bound from the coast of Africa to the Island of Barbadoes, in 1797" (pp. 90-93) involves a slaver which had left Africa with a slave cargo destined for Barbados. Since French privateers infested the African coast, Captain M'Quay "taught his male slaves the use of arms" so that they might assist in repelling any French attack. Instead, some two hundred of the slaves revolted. Twelve crewmen escaped in a small boat, and after a number of days without food, they "soaked their shoes, and two hairy caps . . . in water, and when they had become soft, each partook of them." But as the days passed and as their hunger increased "they fell upon the horrible expedition of eating each other." The survivors, two men and a boy, drifted at sea for some thirty-eight days, and in October 1797 they were discovered on Barbados's east coast by "a Mr. Nascoll, then in the Bay-house of Mr. Haynes" near Joes' River.

"The shipwreck of the sloop Betsy, Philip Aubin, commander. On the coast of Dutch Guiana, the 5th of August, 1756" (pp. 106-21). Captain Aubin relates how he sailed from Barbados to Surinam in a ship owned by Bridgetown merchants. His cargo consisted of provisons and horses; the latter were in such great demand in Surinam that the Dutch passed a law prohibiting English vessels from trading in the colony unless horses were included as part of the cargo. Most of the account details the shipwreck and the suffering of the crew; they finally returned to Barbados, where they were treated by the doctors Hillary and Lilihorn.

PRENTISS, BENJAMIN

The blind African slave or memoirs of Boyrereau Brinch, nick-named Jeffrey Brace.

St. Albans [Vermont], 1810. *204 pp.*   [AAS]

An American abolitionist novel, written as an African's life story narrated by him to the author. Captured in Africa in 1758, the protagonist is transported to Barbados where he landed in 1759 or 1760 and remained several months before being taken to the American colonies. His often lurid description of his sufferings and malevolent treatment by white owners

provide no descriptive materials on Barbados per se, and the geographical setting could be anywhere. Available on microcard in the Early American Imprint Series (second series, no. 21130) from an original copy at the AAS.

THOMAS, ISAIAH

The history of printing in America.

Worcester, 1810. 2 vols.   [JCB]

Materials on Barbados's first printers, Samuel Keimer (who arrived in early 1730 and later died on the island) and his former apprentice David Harry (who came to Barbados in late 1730 but only stayed a few months) are found in both volumes, though these materials frequently derive from Benjamin Franklin's autobiography (see above, Franklin 1793). Although Thomas focuses on the printers' lives while they were in Pennsylvania, there are occasional references to their activities in Barbados (vol. l, pp. 151, 312-20; vol. 2, pp. 33-38, 47-48, 327, 385-86, 512). Keimer is also discussed in a section on the history of the *Barbados Gazette* (the first newspaper in the British West Indies), while another section provides a brief history of the *Barbados Mercury* (vol. 2, pp. 386-89).

THOMPSON, G. A.

The geographical and historical dictionary of America and the West Indies . . . with large additions and compilations from modern voyages and travels.

London, 1812-15. 5 vols.   [JCB]

An enlarged English translation of Antonio de Alcedo y Bejarano, *Diccionario Geografico-Historico de las Indias Occidentales O America* (Madrid, 1786-89 [JCB]). Alcedo y Bejarano's brief and conventional account of Barbados (vol. 1, pp. 134-38), based on published materials, includes information on early colonization and history, physical geography, agricultural products, climate, and government. Thompson supplements this account with a much lengthier one, also based on a variety of sources, which corrects details and offers more information on early colonization, the Courteen-Carlisle controversy, Yarico and Inkle, "Barbados Tar," government, hurricanes, fires, soils, population size, commerce, and exports; 1810 is the latest date mentioned.

DICKSON, WILLIAM

Mitigation of slavery in two parts.

London, 1814. *528 pp.* [JCB]

Dickson's well-known volume is described in JSH-71, but the JCB copy only includes part I, pp. 1-192, "The Letters and Papers of the Late Hon. Joshua Steele." These pages have occasional marginal manuscript notations as well as separate manuscript pages of miscellaneous notes and comments taken from various sources such as newspapers; the manuscript pages are interleaved and bound into the printed pages. Internal evidence makes it plain that the manuscript notations are in Dickson's own hand and were made over several years subsequent to the volume's publication. Although the marginal notes and interleaved pages offer no information on Barbados itself, they are of interest with respect to Dickson and his views on slavery.

YOUNG, SIR WILLIAM

A few poems, written at different periods of my life, now first collected and printed for presentation to friends.

Barbados [1815]. *50 pp.* [BL, NYPL]

Although printed in Barbados (by William Walker and Company), none of these poems deal with the island. The publication year is indicated by paginal watermarks; the title page is dated "government-house, Tobago, March 1814."

BROWN, WILLIAM

The history of the missions; or, of the propagation of Christianity among the heathen.

Philadelphia, 1816. 2 vols. [NYPL]

Based on published sources, this history of the United Brethren (Moravian) missions includes a chapter on the West Indies which, in turn, contains a few pages on Barbados (vol. 1, pp. 388-90); these provide a brief and superficial account of the establishment of the Moravians on the island, the names of the missionaries, numbers baptized, and so forth from 1765 to around 1798.

THE COLONIAL policy of Great Britain, considered with relation to her North American provinces and West India possessions . . . By a British traveller.

London, 1816. *238 pp.* [JCB]

Concerned with the "dangerous tendency of American competition" to Great Britain's trade, the author argues, among other matters, that Britain should encourage more imports from the West Indies by stimulating the latter to produce agricultural products which are now imported from the United States. The West Indies chapter contains a brief discussion (pp. 174-76) of how Barbados could become a source of new (white) farmers for Trinidad. Opposing the view that whites cannot farm in the tropics, the author offers Barbados (where "numerous descendants of the original settlers . . . labour in the field as their fathers did before them") as evidence of this ability; he emphasizes that "prejudice alone clogs the white man's industry, as will appear from the well known fact that robust able-bodied Barbadians will peremptorily refuse to labour in the field, alleging as a reason, that it would be a disgrace to work like a 'Negar.'"

HENDERSON, CAPTAIN

A brief view of the actual condition and treatment of the Negro slaves, in the British Colonies; in a letter to a member of the imperial parliament.

London, 1816. *56 pp.* [JCB]

The author had lived in the West Indies "for some years," starting in 1803, and again visited the area in 1815. Landing in Barbados in 1803, he observed slaving vessels in Carlisle Bay and the auctioning of slaves on shore (pp. 50-51). His brief account mildly deplores what he observed, but emphasizes that since the slave trade's abolition such scenes no longer exist and slaves are now much better treated. This pamphlet was prompted by the controversy surrounding the "slave registry bill"; it generally defends the West Indian planters, the view that slaves are fairly treated, and that their treatment has considerably improved over the years.

RYAN, MICHAEL

A series of letters, published in the Barbados news-papers, commencing from the 11th September, 1815; collected and printed in succession.

Bridgetown, 1816. *88 pp.* [JCB]

In 1815 the Reverend Thomas Allison, of Saint Philip's parish, died, and John Spooner, the president of the Barbados Council, appointed William Als, rector of Saint Thomas, to succeed Allison, and George Maynard, rector of Saint Michael, to succeed Als in Saint Thomas. These appointments generated a controversy, the issues of which are recorded in letters to the editors of various Barbadian newspapers. This rare item, compiled by Ryan, a newspaper editor himself, is useful for Barbados's church history and the relations between the church and political establishments.

ANTIDOTE TO *West-Indian sketches, drawn from authentic sources.*
London, 1816-17.   [JCB]
Tracts designed to refute the emancipationist arguments given in *West-Indian Sketches. Drawn from Authentic Sources* (1816-17). Each tract, usually only a few pages long, has its own pagination and is based on published sources. Barbados and its slave system is occasionally referred to in the following tracts: No. I. *Condition of the slaves in the British colonies, from Pinckard's Notes on the West Indies* (1816, 8 pp.); No. II, *A short account of the African institution* (1816, 8 pp.); No. III, *The actual condition of the Negroes in the British West India colonies* (1816, 8 pp.); No. VI, *Observations on the ameliorated condition of the Negroes in the British West India colonies* (1817, 16 pp.).

WEST-INDIAN SKETCHES. *Drawn from authentic sources.*
London, 1816-17. *84 pp.*   [JCB]
Emancipationist tracts, separately numbered but with a cumulative pagination. Each brief tract focuses on a different subject, but all seem to be based on published materials. Occasional references to slavery in Barbados are in: No. 5, *Anecdotes, tending to elucidate the nature of our colonial bondage* (pp. 41-51), which provide a few excerpts from George Pinckard's *Observations* (1806; JSH-71) on the condition of the island's slaves; and No. 6. *Remarks on the antidote to the West-Indian sketches* (pp. 53-68) which discusses a famous case during the early nineteenth century involving the brutal murder of a slave by whites—not considered a capital offense under contemporary Barbadian law.

BARBADOS ASSEMBLY AND COUNCIL
An act for more fully ascertaining the slave population of the island of Barbados.
[Bridgetown, 1817]. *8 pp.*   [BAN]
One of the more celebrated and controversial of the island's slave laws, the so-called "slave registry bill" was passed on January 9, 1817. Printed at the Barbados printery of William Walker, the BAN catalog (and, following it, the NUC) erroneously identifies "Kingstown" as the place of publication. Printed copies of this act seem to be rare; a manuscript copy is located in the PRO (CO 30/20, no. 343).

GRIFFIN, EDWARD D.
A plea for Africa. A sermon preached October 26, 1817, in the first Presbyterian church in the city of New York.
New York, 1817. *76 pp.*   [H]
A strong indictment of slavery. The explanatory notes, based on secondary sources, include population figures for Barbados slaves, and briefly mention Joseph Rachel, "a free Negro of B'dos" (pp. 42-43, 45).

*LESUEUR, CHARLES ALEXANDRE
"Observations on several species of the genus Actinia illustrated by figures."
Journal of the Academy of Natural Sciences of Philadelphia, 1, 1817, 149-54, 169-87.*
The French naturalist Lesueur visited Barbados in early 1816 (see chapter 3, France) and collected various zoological specimens; his Barbados collection of this genus of sea anemone furnished materials for a large part of this paper (E. T. Hamy, *Les voyages du naturaliste Ch. Alex. Lesueur dans l'Amerique du Nord* [Paris, 1904, p. 14]).

MACLURE, WILLIAM
"Observations on the geology of the West India islands, from Barbadoes to Santa Cruz, inclusive."
Journal of the Academy of Natural Sciences of Philadelphia, 1, 1817, 134-49.   [URB]
A paper originally read before the Academy on October 28, 1817; it includes a brief and superficial description (p. 135) of Barbados's geology. Maclure, an American geologist, was a traveling companion of Charles Alexandre Lesueur (*see* chapter 3, France).

WATSON, RICHARD
A defence of the Wesleyan Methodist missions in the West Indies.
London, 1817. *163 pp.* [JCB, NYPL, NL]
Calling for reform of the slave system and the treatment of slaves, particularly their Christianization, this work was prompted by the 1816 Barbados slave revolt and accusations that Methodist missionaries provoked "that catastrophe." Watson

vigorously denies such charges and argues that the real work of converting slaves was undertaken by missionary groups because the established Church neglected this role. Perhaps partially based on the author's earlier experiences in the West Indies, including Barbados (which is occasionally mentioned), he draws from accounts of missionaries who had lived in the islands. There is a brief description of the social and religious customs of slaves, while lengthier sections give histories of various mission groups and describe the treatment of, and charges against, Methodist missionaries in the West Indies; also, a discussion of the distinctions between Methodists and Moravians and reasons why Methodists are opposed in some parts of the West Indies. In general, a valuable source for Methodist views on slavery and related issues, and the details of missionary work.

BURTON, ALFRED
The adventures of Johnny Newcome in the Navy. A poem in four cantos.
London, 1818. *259 pp.*   [BL]
The BL catalog identifies the real author as John Mitford. A very long fictional account of a young sailor in the British Navy. By including this item in his *Barbados poetry: A check list* (Mona, Jamaica: Savacou, 1979), Edward Brathwaite misleads for the item has nothing to do with Barbados. The island is only mentioned in one line of this several-hundred page, poem, viz. "without encountering tornadoes/ John saw Madeira and Barbadoes . . . ." Also located at Yale University. A print in the Barbados Museum, *Barbados, Newcombe and Mrs. Sambo,* may be related to this item (JSH-71, p. 119, no. 9).

WALKER, JAMES
Letters on the West Indies.
London, 1818. *268 pp.*   [JCB]
A property owner in the West Indies years, Walker was prompted to write this book by the controversy surrounding the "slave registry bill." Written from the perspective of a reformist who is also sympathetic to the planters, he ranges over a variety of topics, such as,"the interference of the British public in colonial affairs," "the capability of the British public to judge colonial affairs," the slave system and slave treatment, the effects of Christianity on slaves, and "on the African character."

Although references are usually to the West Indies in general, occasionally specific islands are mentioned. Brief comments on Barbados note the sea passage to Jamaica (p. 33), Moravian missions (p. 35), Joshua Steele and the management of his slaves (pp. 52, 68), the Christianization of slaves (p. 105, 107-9, 138), free coloreds (p. 172), and the 1816 slave revolt (p. 215).

JACKSON, ROBERT
A sketch of the history and cure of febrile diseases; more particularly as they appear in the West Indies among the soldiers of the British Army.
London, 1820. 2 vols.   [BL]
At the time of writing, the author was a retired British Army doctor. This "second edition, with many additions" includes a new section (not included in the first, 1817, edition) on military positions, barracks, and hospitals in the British West Indies between 1812 and 1815. This section (vol. 2) provides a general introduction to disease-producing factors in the West Indies (with occasional specific references to Barbados), and subsequently treats each island individually. The pages on Barbados (252-64) describe the island's water supplies, climate, and major diseases, but focus on the barracks at St. Ann's Garrison, the size of buildings, their construction, design, and so forth; there are also a few case histories of soldiers afflicted with one disease or another.

Three tables in vol. 2 also provide information on Barbados. Table 1 (following p. 232) individually lists each British Caribbean territory by year (over the period 1803-14) and race of the troops (black and white), and provides information on the number of soldiers admitted and discharged from army hospitals, the number of deaths, proportion of deaths to numbers discharged, and proportion of deaths to the number of troops. Tables 2 and 3 are specifically concerned with the Barbados garrison. Table 2 (following p. 238) provides monthly data for 1831 by race on the number of troops, the names and size of their units, the number and principal diseases of the sick, the number of deaths from each type of disease, the total discharged, and the number of deaths during the year; explanatory notes (pp. 239-40) accompany the table. Table 3 (following p. 240) provides the same information, but for the year 1814 (explanatory notes are on pp. 241-42). In all, an excellent source for the issues with which it deals.

JORDAN, GIBBES WALKER
On the floatage of small heavy bodies in air, and certain atmospheric phenomena dependent thereon.
London, 1820.   [BL]
See Jordan 1799 *(Account of the Irides).*

MAYCOCK, JAMES DOTTIN
A sermon, preached at the parish church of St. Michael, Barbados, on the 19th of March, 1820, on the death of our late sovereign.
Barbados [1820]. *33 pp.*   [JCB]
Contains nothing about Barbados. The author was rector of St. Michael. Rare.

BARBADOS DISTRICT COMMITTEE
Rules and regulations of the Barbados District Committee.
[Bridgetown, 1821?]. *2 pp.*   [UWI]
An apparently rare item, these rules of the Society for Promoting Christian Knowledge were adopted on January 18, 1821, at a meeting at the Central School. The name of the Barbados District Committee was later changed to the Barbados Diocesan Committee.

BARBADOS SOCIETY FOR PROMOTING CHRISTIAN KNOWLEDGE
[Fourth] report of the Barbados Society for Promoting Christian Knowledge.
Barbados, 1823. *8 pp.*   [UWI]
See Barbados Society for Promoting Christian Knowledge, 1828.

CUFFY, THE Negro's doggerel description of the progress of sugar.
London [1823]. *34 pp.*   [JCB]
In what the author purports to be "black talk," this work describes various stages of sugar production, for example, "holeing," "manuring," "planting," each stage being described in a short verse and illustrated by a colored drawing. Barbados is only mentioned once (p. 8) in a section on "guarding" that is typical of the style: "That thing call'd a hedge you no see in B'adoes/ Cow, and sheep, and pig, if not tied invade us/ When the cane be ripe some one steal too much-ee/So with lance and sword night and day we watch-ee." No date of

publication is given, but the pages are watermarked 1823.

ROSE, G. H.
A letter on the means and importance of converting the slaves in the West Indies to Christianity.
London, 1823. *87 pp.*   [JCB]
A member of Parliament, the author's major argument for Christianizing slaves is his conviction that the Gospel will lead them "to rational obedience, order, industry, and morality . . . to things innocent and useful." Written when there was increasing controversy in Britain over slave emancipation, the author opines that "the effusions of our licentious press cannot but reach them, and produce the most mischievous effects unless sound instruction counteract its poison, or induce them to reject it." Barbados is occasionally mentioned in the appendix which contains several extracts of 1817 and 1822 letters reporting on Anglican activities among the slaves, and a few materials on the Methodists for whom Barbados "has ever been the least successful of our West Indian missions" (pp. 48-49, 72-73, 75-76, 77).

WILBERFORCE, WILLIAM
An appeal to the religion, justice, and humanity of the inhabitants of the British Empire, in behalf of the Negro slaves in the West Indies.
London, 1823. *77 pp.*   [JCB]
The celebrated emancipationist's analysis of slavery and plea to end it "as soon as it may be safely done." Barbados is mentioned in several places with reference to the island's slave laws, comments on the status of free persons of color, Joshua Steele; there is also a relatively lengthy discussion on the murder of slaves being a noncapital offense (pp. 11, 21-22, 38-39, 54-62).

BARBADOS ASSEMBLY AND COUNCIL
An act to amend and render more effectual an act entitled, "an act the better to enable the several vestries of the . . . parishes of St. Michael, Christ Church, Saint James, and Saint Peter . . . to tax new-comers and non-residents trading there, towards their parish charges.
[Barbados, 1824]. *2 pp.*   [JCB]
Receiving the governor's assent on June 4, 1824, this separately printed act modifies

one passed in 1722. The present act notes evasion of the 1722 law by "new-comers and non-residents"; in order to avoid an import tax, they bring their goods into Barbados for sale by pretending that they have been regularly consigned to resident Barbadians.

FORM OF divine service for the Negroes. Adopted by the meeting of the clergy and planters.

[Barbados, 1824?].

I have been unable to locate a copy of this item. It was advertised in *The Barbadian* newspaper, January 3, 1824, as being on sale at the paper's office in Bridgetown.

*HARTE, REVEREND WILLIAM MARSHALL

A sermon (preached in the parish church of St. Lucy in this island) entitled "slavery not inconsistent with Christianity."

[Bridgetown, 1824].

On January 3, 1824, the *Barbadian* newspaper notified its readership that this sermon was about to be published, and on February 25, 1824, the "pamphlet" was advertised for sale; at the time, Harte was rector of St. Lucy. For other works relating to slavery by Harte, see JSH-71 and Harte 1830, below.

HINTS ON the propriety of establishing by law the civil rights of the free people of colour in the British West India colonies.

Newcastle Upon Tyne, 1824. *14 pp.* [BM]

Argues for extending civil rights, delineates legal disabilities, and suggests the qualifications by which free coloreds "might become entitled to full participation of civil rights," as well as various criteria that should be employed in emancipating the slaves. The writer speaks of Barbados "from his own observation," and although the island is only specifically mentioned once, his argument implicitly applies to Barbados.

BARBADOS SOCIETY FOR PROMOTING CHRISTIAN KNOWLEDGE

Sixth annual report of the Barbados Society for the Promotion of Christian Knowledge.

[Barbados], 1825. *8 pp.* [UWI]

See Barbados Society for Promoting Christian Knowledge, 1828.

BRANCH ASSOCIATION OF THE ISLAND OF BARBADOS, IN AID OF THE INCORPORATED SOCIETY FOR THE CONVERSION AND RELIGIOUS IN- STRUCTION AND EDUCATION OF THE NEGRO SLAVES IN THE BRITISH WEST INDIA ISLANDS

First annual report of the Branch Association of the Island of Barbados in aid of the Incorporated Society.

Bridgetown, 1826. *24 pp.* [UWI]

Despite the occasional efforts of individual clergymen in earlier years, the report notes that "no system was publicly adopted" by the Church of England for the religious instruction of slaves until August 1823; two years later the Branch Association was formally organized. This report sketches the origin and development of slave missionary work by the Anglican Church, and the formation of the Society for the Conversion and Religious Instruction. The bulk of the report, however, is a parish-by- parish review, based on the reports of parochial rectors, of activities in each parish with respect to slave religious instruction. Information is provided on, for example, the number of plantations and other properties where slaves are being instructed, the subjects they are taught, how this teaching is approached, and the number of times each property is visited by a catechist. An apparently rare item. Later activities of the Branch Association can be found in the *Annual Reports* issued by the mother Society and published in London (JSH-71, p. 75).

EDINBURGH SOCIETY FOR PROMOTING THE MITIGATION AND ULTIMATE ABOLITION OF NEGRO SLAVERY

The second annual report of the Edinburgh Society.

Edinburgh, 1825. *43 pp.* [JCB]

Occasional references to Barbados include critisicms of legislative reforms to the island's slave laws (pp. 8, 21-24), bitter reactions to the 1823 destruction of the Methodist chapel and the missionary's forced departure, including a strident reprimand of "the Christian whites of Barbadoes"(pp. 9-10, 11), and comments on the size of the slave population (pp. 31, 33).

SAMPLES OF *slavery*.
London [ca. 1825]. *4 pp.*   [JCB]
An emancipationist tract. Among items dealing with various West Indian colonies, it includes a brief excerpt from the Barbados slave code.

BARBADOS SOCIETY FOR PROMOTING CHRISTIAN KNOWLEDGE
[Seventh] report of the Barbados Society for Promoting Christian Knowledge.
Bridgetown, 1826. *10 pp.*   [UWI]
See Barbados Society for Promoting Christian Knowledge, 1828.

LADIES' ASSOCIATION FOR RELIEVING THE INDIGENT SICK OF BRIDGETOWN
First annual report of the Ladies' Association for Relieving the Indigent Sick of Bridge-Town, and its Environs.
[Bridgetown, 1826]. *2 pp.*   [UWI]
One of several charitable organizations formed during this period, the Ladies' Association was established in September, 1825, and seems to have been entirely composed of white women whose endeavors were solely directed toward the white poor. This report (a broadside bound as two leaves) delineates the Association's objectives "for those in the greatest need," viz., to provide a daily meal as well as a small weekly allowance of candles, sugar, and "other comforts." The report describes the meals and other services, and the association's organizational format, operating rules, sources of funds, and so forth. An apparently rare item. For a history of this association, see Neville Connell's article in *JBMHS*, 24, 1957, 53-65.

M'DONNELL, ALEXANDER
The West India legislatures vindicated from the charge of having resisted the call of the mother country for the amelioration of slavery.
London 1826. *104 pp.*   [JCB]
Defends the colonial legislatures against accusations that they are resisting emancipation and only confining themselves to reform of slavery. Trinidad is frequently mentioned, and other West Indian territories are occasionally discussed; Barbados's newly passed "consolidated slave act" is briefly noted as is slave baptisms and marriages on the island (pp. 43-44, 54-55).

BARBADOS ASSEMBLY AND COUNCIL
Barbados. An act for vesting a certain piece or parcel of land in the governors, directors and members of the "Barbados Society for Promoting Christian Knowledge" and their successors, and for altering the name and style of the said society.
[Barbados, 1827]. *3 pp.*   [UWI]
Assented to by the governor in May 1827, this act grants two and one-half acres to the Society for Promoting Christian Knowledge, and changes the name of the society to the Barbados Society for the Education of the Poor in the Principles of the Established Church. A school for white girls was to be built on the land, and appended is a surveyor's diagram of the plot showing the lands and names of landowners on which it bounded.

BARBADOS DIOCESAN COMMITTEE OF THE SOCIETY FOR PROMOTING CHRISTIAN KNOWLEDGE
Report of the Barbados Diocesan Committee of the Society for Promoting Christian Knowledge.
Bridgetown, 1827. *17 pp.*   [UWI]
Earlier called the Barbados District Committee of the Society for Promoting Christian Knowledge, this report notes that the committee had not issued an earlier report because "for a considerable period" it was only regarded "as a subsidiary branch of the Central School," a school in Bridgetown for poor white children (established in 1819 and operated and sponsored by the Society for Promoting Christian Knowledge). Observing that the Central School has had marked progress since its inception, the Diocesan Committee feels it can "no longer refrain from laying before the public the success of their labours." The report reviews the history of the Barbados S.P.C.K., how it became affiliated with the S.P.C.K. in England, and how, on January 18, 1821, the Barbados District Committee was formally established. The subsequent history of the Barbados S.P.C.K. is given, as well as its finances, relationship to the Central School, and rules of the committee. Also included are statistical information on the committee's affairs and the number of religious tracts and books it distributed from 1824 through 1827. An apparently rare item.

BARBADOS SOCIETY FOR PROMOTING CHRISTIAN KNOWLEDGE
Eighth annual report of the Barbados Society for Promoting Christian Knowledge.
Bridgetown, 1827. *20 pp.* [UWI]
See Barbados Society for Promoting Christian Knowledge, 1828.

BARRALLIER, F.
To his excellency . . . Lord Combermere . . . and to Gibbes Walker Jordan . . . this trigonometrical survey . . . [of Barbados] is most respectfully dedicated.
London, 1827. [JCB, BL]
A large (147 cm x 118 cm) and detailed topographic map, engraved in 1825. Among other features, the map locates plantations, and its lower corners contain a printed list of approximately 425 plantations and "places," with their parish locations and owners' names.

LADIES' ASSOCIATION FOR RELIEVING THE INDIGENT SICK OF BRIDGETOWN
Second annual report of the Ladies' Association for the Relief of the Indigent Sick and Infirm of Bridge-Town, and its Environs.
Bridgetown, 1827. *9 pp.* [UWI]
This second report of the Ladies' Association (see also, above, Ladies' Association 1826) gives more details than the first on the number of people served by the association, as well as an overview of services provided, the association's financial state, and the ways in which monies are raised. Appended to this report (although it *may* have been published separately in 1825 or 1826) is the association's three-page "Rules and Regulations." As with the first report, this one is also apparently rare.

LADIES' BRANCH ASSOCIATION FOR THE EDUCATION OF FEMALE CHILDREN OF THE COLOURED POOR
First annual report of the Ladies' Branch Association for the Education of Female Children of the Coloured Poor on the Principles of the Established Church of England.
Bridgetown, 1827. *16 pp.* [UWI]
Established in October 1826 and composed of free colored women, the Branch Association was formed to assist the Society for the Education of the Coloured Poor in the Principles of the Established Church (1827). This society was to establish and support a separate Charity School for free colored and slave girls where their religious and academic instruction would be supplemented by learning "useful needle-work." The report reviews the history of the Branch Association, its current financial status, and the size of its student population. Appended is a three-page "Rules and Regulations" of the association as well as a list of its governing committee and financial supporters.

This apparently rare item is a valuable source of information on the organizational life of the free colored community (i.e., freedman), the names of its members (particularly women), and the early establishment of educational institutions for free coloreds and slaves.

NORIE, JOHN WILLIAM
West India directory, containing instructions for navigating the Caribbee . . . islands
London, 1827. Pt. I. *46 pp.* [BL]
As indicated in the title, navigational instructions. A little more than a page (pp. 13-14) treats Barbados and includes geographical descriptions of landmarks seen as approaching the island and detailed instructions for navigating Carlisle Bay and anchoring in it; a few similar details are given on Speightstown.

SOCIETY FOR THE EDUCATION OF THE COLOURED POOR IN THE PRINCIPLES OF THE ESTABLISHED CHURCH
First annual report of the Society for the Education of the Coloured Poor in the Principles of the Established Church, and for other Charitable Relief.
Bridgetown, 1827. *16 pp.* [UWI]
Paralleling the white-membership Barbados Society for the Education of the Poor in the Principles of the Established Church, which was concerned with educating poor white children at the Central School in Bridgetown, the Society for the Education of the Coloured Poor was founded in September, 1826, by members of the free colored (i.e., freedman) community. It was an outgrowth and consolidation of three earlier free colored charitable organizations: The Colonial Charity School; the Ancient Samaritan Society (or, the Samaritan Charitable Society); and the Friendly Association for Clothing. The

Society for the Education of the Coloured Poor had as its objectives the "religious education of the coloured poor, clothing the naked, feeding the hungry, and giving Christian interment to the deceased." With assistance from the Church Missionary Society in London, the society also operated the Colonial Charity School in Bridgetown. Established in 1818 for free colored and slave boys and girls, the school was not only Barbados's first public school for nonwhites but also the first institution of its kind in the West Indies.

The report reviews the society's and, particularly, the Colonial Charity School's history, mentions the names of leading whites who helped support the school, reviews the society's finances, gives the number of slave and free colored pupils, and the number of persons who received other forms of support, including interment. The report also names the society's governing committee which included about twenty-nine free colored men; various prominent whites (for example, the Governor, Lord Bishop, Archdeacon) held honorific titles. Appended to the report is a two-page list of financial contributors to the society for the year September 1826-September 1827 and the amount each donated—about ninety persons, most of whom appear to be free coloreds.

Along with other materials (see JSH-71, pp. 70, 137) this rare item is an important source of information on the early establishment in Barbados of educational institutions for nonwhites; it is also of special interest for the composition of the free colored community, especially its leading male members, and the nature of the community's organizational life.

BARBADOS SOCIETY FOR PROMOTING CHRISTIAN KNOWLEDGE

Ninth annual report of the Barbados Society for the Education of the Poor in the Principles of the Established Church.
Bridgetown, 1828. *15 pp.*   [UWI]
The fourth, sixth, seventh, eighth, and ninth annual reports, most of which are apparently rare, are located at UWI. Copies of the seventh and ninth are also located in the United States, but were not previously consulted; several later reports of the society are also known to exist (see JSH-71, pp. 72, 80). UWI also contains manuscript copies of the first (6 pp.) and fifth (8 pp.)

reports, written in 1820 and 1824, respectively, and bound in with the published reports; it is unknown if the 1820 and 1824 reports were ever published.

Formed in 1818 and affiliated with the English S.P.C.K. in the following year, the Barbados S.P.C.K. (sometimes referred to as the Society for the Promotion of Christian Knowledge, but usually as the Society for Promoting Christian Knowledge) was principally established to provide "a more efficient system of education among the [white] lower classes" (JSH-71, p. 71). In 1827, the name of the Barbados S.P.C.K. was formally changed by legislative action (see above, Barbados Assembly and Council, 1827) to the Barbados Society for the Education of the Poor in the Principles of the Established Church. The *Ninth Annual Report* was the first issued under the new name; and until at least 1835 the annual reports continued to be issued under this name (JSH-71, p. 72).

The following summary is based on both the printed and manuscript reports listed above. The principal function of the Barbados S. P. C. K. was raising funds for, and operating, the Central School in Bridgetown. This had been established by 1819 "to afford religious and suitable education to poor white children" of both sexes by educating them in "the principles of religion and morality," and by "forming them to habits of industry" through teaching religious subjects, reading, writing, arithmetic (and, later, English grammar); in addition, the girls learned sewing and the boys such skills as shoemaking and repair and bookbinding. An ultimate objective of the school was to send out as apprentices to various occupations the pupils who finished the course of studies. Boys and girls attended the same school as day pupils or as boarders until August, 1826, when a separate Central School for girls was constructed and commenced operations.

The annual reports detail the progress of the schools by providing miscellaneous comments and information, including: observations on the conduct of, and problems with, pupils; attendance; the numbers apprenticed out, and, occasionally their names and trades; school finances and funding sources; and dismissals for failure to conform to behavioral standards. Also occasionally given are the names of teachers and of the governing board and officers. The *Eighth Annual Report* is especially detailed on a variety of matters not included, or only partially treated, in other reports. It provides a summary history of the Barbados S. P. C. K. since its formation, and outlines why it was started, the school's origin, and from where the earliest pupils were drawn. There is also a detailed discussion of sources of funding, annual expenses for the food, clothing, books, and medical care of pupils, and details on the organization and format of both schools, the subjects taught, the daily schedule, food and clothing allowances to pupils, and so forth. The eighth report also includes a plan of the boy's school showing its physical layout as well as describing its interior.

In all, these reports constitute a valuable source of information on the early establishment of formal educational institutions in Barbados.

[MACGREGOR, DUNCAN]
  A narrative of the loss of the ship Kent, by fire, in the Bay of Biscay, on the first of March, 1825.
  Bridgetown, 1828. *41 pp.*
Located at the Hamilton College Library (Clinton, New York), this is a very rare Barbados reprint of 1825 Edinburgh editions (BL, NYPL), none of which contain materials on the West Indies. (For a connection between the loss of the *Kent* and Barbados see *JBMHS*, 30, 1962, 26.)

COLERIDGE, WILLIAM HART
  An address delivered to the candidates for holy orders in the diocese of Barbados and the Leeward islands; and other addresses.
  London, 1829. *207 pp.*
Included in JSH-71, but somewhat misleadingly described. This item actually comprises five separately printed tracts, bound together into the volume located in the library of the Barbados Museum and Historical Society. The indivdual tracts are held by various libraries (see GIL). The author was the Bishop of Barbados. Some of his many publications are listed in JSH-71, and a few are also listed in this *Supplement*. GIL, however, discusses a number of other works and should be consulted by any researcher interested in Coleridge's published writings.

*[COLERIDGE, WILLIAM HART]
  An address in two parts, delivered at a private confirmation in the Cathedral, 29th September, 1829.
  Bridgetown, 1829. *15 pp.*   [O-BO]
By the Bishop of Barbados; citation and location from GIL and *NSTC.*

*[COLERIDGE, WILLIAM HART]
  A Letter.
  Bridgetown, 1829. *15 pp.*   [O-BO]
From the Bishop of Barbados to the clergy of his diocese; see GIL.

HOLMES, ABIEL
  The annals of America, from the discovery by Columbus . . . to the year 1826.
  Cambridge, Mass., 1829. 2nd ed. 2 vols.
                                        [JCB]
In 1698 Nathaniel Williams "was ordained in the college hall at Cambridge [Mass.] to take the pastoral charge of a noncomformist church at Barbadoes" (vol. 1, p. 469). The first edition was published in 1805 (Cambridge, Mass.).

OBSERVATIONS ON the progress of the Episcopal establishment in the West Indies.
  London, 1829. *35 pp.*   [JCB]
Focusing on the diocese of Barbados, this is a sympathetic discussion and evaluation of the Anglican church, its newly appointed bishop, and the Church's activities, including those among slaves.

SMYTH, WILLIAM HENRY
  The life and services of Captain Philip Beaver, late of His Majesty's Ship Nisus.
  London, 1829. *340 pp.*   [NL, NYPL]
Beaver visited Barbados several times during 1807-1809 (pp. 164, 169-70, 183, 192) while his ship was being provisioned, usually prior to major expeditions against the French. Nothing is said about these visits other than mentioning that during one of them about twenty of his crew became afflicted with a "fever," some even dying.

AN ABSTRACT of the British West Indian statutes, for the protection and government of slaves.
  London, 1830. *43 pp.*   [BL]
Published by the Standing Committee of West Indian Planters and Merchants in London in order to show "what the colonial legislatures have *actually done* towards the amelioration of slavery";

includes brief summaries of two major Barbados slave laws assented to by the Crown in October, 1827 (pp. 8-10): the "slave consolidation act" and the "Sunday and marriage act."

*HARTE, REVEREND WILLIAM MARSHALL
Pastoral duties, taken in connection with the state of the West India Islands.
Barbados, 1830.   [CU?]
The author and imprint data are taken from "The Rev. William Harte and Attitudes to Slavery in Early Nineteenth-Century Barbados" *(Journal of Ecclesiastical History,* 30, 1979, 471) by J. T. Gilmore who writes that this item contains a sermon to the Barbados diocese clergy "recommending not only the religious instruction of slaves, but even that they should be taught to read." A search of the CU library catalog in June 1984 as well as the catalogs of several other major libraries in the U.S. and Great Britain failed to locate a copy. CU, however, has a copy of Harte's *Practical Sermons* (London, 1839) which, according to Gilmore (p. 471), "contains nothing of specifically West Indian interest." For other works relating to slavery by the rector of St. Lucy parish, see JSH-71 and Harte 1824, above.

PORTER, GEORGE RICHARDSON
The nature and properties of the sugar cane; with practical directions for the improvement of its culture, and the manufacture of its products.
London, 1830. *390 pp.*   [JCB, BL]
An erudite and detailed treatise on cane cultivation and sugar and rum manufacture; Barbados is sometimes specifically mentioned. Pages 324-28 include an "estimate" of an unnamed Barbados plantation, giving detailed information on such items as expenses, acreage, type, quantity, and value of agricultural products, the number of livestock and slaves, as well as the expenses of feeding and clothing the latter. A second London edition was published in 1843 [BL].

*WILKINSON, CHARLES HENRY
An enquiry into the natural history, chemical properties and medical virtues of the rock oil . . . of Barbadoes.
London, 1830.   [BL]

COLERIDGE, WILLIAM HART
A selection of psalms and hymns, . . . with appropriate tunes. Recommended for the use of the cathedral and other churches and chapels in the Diocese of Barbados and the Leeward islands.
Barbados, 1831. *100 pp.*   [BL]
Contents as indicated in the title; collected by the Bishop of Barbados.

VINDEX
The conduct of the British Government towards the Church of England in the West India colonies: in a letter to Viscount Goderich.
London, 1831. *24 pp.*   [JCB]
Antiabolitionist and critical of George Murray, Goderich's predecessor as Secretary of State for the Colonies, this tract contains a few specific references to Barbados.

HENDY, T[HOMAS] W. B.
An attempt to prove the fallacy of inflicting corporal punishment to prevent or to lessen the commission of crime, and the propriety of immediately restricting it to slave women.
Bridgetown, 1833. *47 pp.*   [JCB]
Signed and dated "The Hermitage [St. Peter], January 1, 1833," this rare work was authored by a Barbadian-born planter. Hendy maintains that it is time for planters "to yield up the right . . . they possess, as slave holders, to inflict of their own will on their delinquent slaves, even the slight floggings they now do"; corporal punishment is not needed for the maintenance of the "strictest discipline" and it "is a debasing punishment which, by its demoralizing effect, causes an increase in crime." He argues for a management system which involves, on the one hand, solitary confinement for punishment and, on the other, food and clothing rewards for good work and behavior; he does not argue for emancipation, but how to better treat the slaves and still maximize their labor.

IRVING, EDWARD
A statement of the cause which affects the decrease or increase of the slave population in the British colonies.
London, 1833. *44 pp.*   [JCB]
Counters the abolitionist position that decrease in West Indian slave populations results from slavery per se, and asserts that in every British island the slave populations

"are now gradually increasing." The argument is elaborated through statistics from official reports, *Parliamentary Papers*, etc., for West Indian slaves during the slave registry triennia. Pages 5, 11-12, 27, and 41 mention or discuss Barbados.

WASHINGTON, GEORGE
> *The writings of George Washington . . . selected and published from the original manuscripts.*
> Boston, 1833-37. 12 vols.   [SIU]

Edited by Jared Sparks. George Washington accompanied his brother Lawrence to Barbados in 1751. Volume 2 (pp. 422, 424-27) contains a brief letter from Lawrence Washington, written from Barbados, and excerpts from George Washington's journal entries during his visit to the island. See also JSH-71, pp. 176-77 for other editions of Washington's diaries. The most recent (not mentioned in JSH-71) is edited by Donald Jackson, *The Diaries of George Washington*, 2 vols. (Charlottesville, University Press of Virginia, 1976); the section relating to Barbados is in volume 1, pages 24 ff.

LEWIS, MATTHEW GREGORY
> *Journal of a West India proprietor, kept during a residence in the island of Jamaica.*
> London, 1834. *408 pp.*   [BL]

This classic of the West Indian literature contains a brief passage (p. 21) on Barbados describing the techniques employed for catching the island's "great multitudes" of flying fish; information on fishing techniques during the slave period is relatively scarce.

STUART, ABEL
> *A statement of facts.*
> London, [1834 or 1835]. *48 pp.*   [BL]

Written by a medical doctor with long experience in Barbados. In discussing the medical histories of several white Barbadian patients, he attempts to provide evidence for the effectiveness of a medicine he has developed for "the removal and cure of cancerous tumours and dangerous excrescences on the human body."

ORDERSON, J. W.
> *The fair Barbadian and faithful black; or, a cure for the gout. A comedy in three acts.*
> Liverpool, 1835. *36 pp.*   [BL]

An apparently rare item and evidently unknown to students of Barbados social history, this play was written by the white creole author of the much better known novel *Creoleana* and several nonfiction works (see JSH-71). First performed in Barbados in 1832, Orderson decided to publish his play in England soon after emancipation, in order to publicize to the British public "through some incidents of fiction and others of fact the real existing relations between master and slave previous to the new principles of connection just established between them," and to stress how this relationship offers a "fair promise of the confidence that may henceforth be mutually reposed by each in the other."

The play, set in Barbados in the 1830s, has eight main characters: seven white, including the central character of a wealthy planter, and Hampshire, the planter's "confidential black servant" who also has a prominent role. The cast includes blacks playing plantation slaves, some of whom have small speaking parts. A series of mishaps befall the planter and his family, and Hampshire, portrayed as the quintessential stereotype of a faithful domestic slave, helps his master out of personal difficulties for which, at the play's end, Hampshire is rewarded with his freedom. Initially rejecting the offer out of loyalty to his master and concern for his own future welfare and material security, Hampshire is relieved that "good provision for your future comfort" has been made, and is lectured on his responsibilities as a free person. Although Hampshire is sceptical that freedom will, in fact, involve equality with his master, the latter assures him that he will still "have duties to perform" and lectures him on "obedience to the laws, and conforming your mind to the principles of Christianity, . . . for you must ever bear in mind that no society can exist without subordination; or its members be happy without religion."

Whatever the value of this play as a literary piece, it is an interesting reflection of the ideology held by liberal white Barbadians during the twilight of slavery. Although the play presents the perspective of one Barbadian creole and how he viewed the character and temperament of his black and white countrymen, it also reflects how many upper stratum whites chose to present themselves and their society to themselves and to outsiders, particularly with respect to slavery and the relationship between masters and slaves—major themes of the play. The play stresses that slave masters are basically kind and responsible persons who maintain a paternalistic relationship with their slaves, provide for their basic needs, and treat them fairly and well. Although masters, occasionally "acting under the combined influence of climate and disease [might be] excited to momentary acts of tyranny," these outbursts "instantly yield to a more amicable nature." Slaves, in turn, are contented and loyal; they not only acknowledge their dependency on their masters for material and other security, but also are grateful for the treatment they receive. To be sure, slaves require discipline, as a child requires discipline from a parent, but slavery is not the cruel and oppressive system conceived by the British emancipationists. The latter hold a greatly distorted view of West Indian slavery, and slave life is far less precarious than the life of British workers—all of which were very common themes in the nonfictional proslavery literature of the period, and which were also expressed by Orderson in several earlier nonfictional works.

The play also contains occasional references to plantation customs and the habits of the plantocracy, and reflects commonly held views of the proper and expected roles and behavior of white creole women. Since blacks play such a central role, a great deal of black speech is transcribed; this is especially valuable for the student of creole languages since the play provides the lengthiest passages extant of black speech behavior recorded by a Barbadian during the slave period.

*[COLERIDGE, WILLIAM HART]

Temporalia, or, instructions for the clergy, relative to ordination, institution to archdeaconries, and benefices . . . etc. etc. in the diocese of Barbados and the Leeward islands.

Barbados [1836]. *24 pp.*   [O-BO]

Imprint data and location are in *NSTC* and GIL; the latter also provides author identification, and notes this item by the Bishop of Barbados is a "compilation of formulae and legal requirements."

[MACAULAY, ZACHARY]

Détails sur l'émancipation des esclaves dans les colonies Anglaises, pendant les années 1834 et 1835, tirés des documens officiels présentés au Parlement Anglais et imprimé par son ordre, avec des observations et des notes par Z. Macaulay, F.R.S. de Londres. Traduit d'Anglais..

Paris, 1836. *128 pp.*   [BL, LC]

Composed of documents extracted from the *Parliamentary Papers, Documents Relative to the Abolition of Slavery* (JSH-71, p. 114), and printed by the House of Commons on April 16 and June 10, 1835. This volume was brought into print because of the French debate on slave emancipation in their colonies, and a consideration of the implications of emancipation by viewing the British colonial experience. Sections treat Jamaica, British Guiana, Mauritius, and Barbados (pp. 41-51), the last involving a few letters from Governor Lionel Smith to the Secretary of State for the Colonies on the issue of emancipation. A companion volume, *Suite des détails sur l'emancipation des esclaves . . . annéés 1834 et 1835* (Paris, 1836, [JCB]), deals with the remaining British West Indian islands. Explanatory notes are given by Macaulay, a leading British abolitionist.

*BRIGGS, JOHN

[To the agricultural peasantry of Barbados.]
Guernsey [1838 or 1839].

Extensive search has failed to yield a copy of this item which is mentioned as follows in the extracts of *The Barbadian* newspaper for February 23, 1839 (*JBMHS*, 8, 1940, 89): "The editor mentions the publication of a book by John Briggs addressed to the Agricultural Peasantry of Barbados; for sale by S. & J. Inniss . . . . It was printed in Guernsey." A John Briggs was an apparently prominent landholder in St. Joseph in the early nineteenth century (he had donated land for the site of a new parish church and held a commission in the militia), but I am not sure if he and the above author were the same person (see *JBMHS*, 8, 1941, 121; 17, 1950, 118).

*EDGHILL, THOMAS

West Indian veterinary medicine.
[Barbados? 1839?].

Reported in *The Barbadian* newspaper for June 15, 1839 (*JBMHS*, 8, 1940, 93):

"Thomas Edghill, 24 Suttle Street, advertises *A Treatise on Veterinary Medicine*, a pocket volume compiled by himself and now in the press." H. A. Vaughan cites the June 6 and 10, 1839 *West Indian* newspaper which gives the title and notes this work gives "special reference to the diseases of horses"; Edghill "was a wholesale saddler" with a business in High Street who later became a farrier in Barbados (*JBMHS*, 22, 1955, 121). Search for this item has failed to yield a copy.

MARTIN, ROBERT MONTGOMERY

Statistics of the colonies of the British Empire in the West Indies . . . . from the official records of the Colonial Office.

London, 1839. *906 pp.*   [NYPL, BL]

Includes (pp. 60-68) an overview of Barbados's political history (with a list of governors up to 1836) and brief descriptions of its political, governmental, and educational systems, as well as its geography and climate. Also there are statistics on: population; number of slaves from 1817 to 1832; births, marriages, and burials for 1832 and 1833; the church establishment; jail prisoners (and associated data) for 1829-32; schools in 1834; and trade, imports, and exports. This was "reissued in 1843 under the title *History of the Colonies of the British Empire*" (*NUC*); for similar earlier works by Martin, see JSH-71.

INKLE & YARICO, a legend of Barbados. By a Barbadian.

[Barbados, ca. 1840s]. *15 pp.*   [AAS]

One of a number of literary by-products of the tale first related by Richard Ligon in 1657 and then more widely publicized by Richard Steele in *The Spectator* of London (JSH-71, p. 21). This long poem is apparently rare. It was "sold by I. Bowen, Bookseller, Broadstreet." Although undated, its printing style clearly indicates publication after the early nineteenth century. The Barbadian-born Israel Bowen opened a "bookseller's shop" on Church Street in 1834; between the latter part of 1838 and 1840 or 1841, the shop moved to Trafalgar Street, and by at least 1846 it was on Broad Street, where Bowen continued selling, as well as publishing, books until 1866 when his firm became I. Bowen and Sons (*JBMHS*, 5, 1938, 207; 7, 1940, 135; 8, 1940, 10, 65; 10, 1943, 145; 28, 1961, 82, 145). Thus, this poem appears to have

been published prior to 1866 and probably around the time, or after, Bowen moved to Broad Street in the 1840s. Although it appears to have been published too late by criteria used for inclusion in this *Supplement,* it is included here on the chance it was published earlier and by a different printer.

EASEL, THEODORE

Desultory sketches and tales of Barbados.

London, 1840. *264 pp.*   [BMHS]

Described in JSH-71. Although the author identifies himself as Easel, he implies that the name is a pseudonym. In the *Barbadian* newspaper for February 6, 1841, the editor "notices publication lately in London of a book entitled Desultory Sketches of Barbados by a much respected country man, an M.C.P. [Member of Colonial Parliament], but whether he is in this island or absent we must not say." Members of the Assembly who were absent at the time were Dr. Francis Goding and Nathaniel Foderinhgam (*JBMHS* ,9, 1942, 185-86); the author of *Desultory Sketches* was probably one of these men.

BURNLEY, WILLIAM HARDIN

Observations on the present condition of the island of Trinidad, and the actual state of the experiment of Negro emancipation.

London, 1842. *171 pp.*   [BL]

Includes the testimony of Samuel J. Prescod (pp. 86-89), who first visited Trinidad in 1840, and whose comparative observations on the work routines and conditions of Barbados plantation laborers sometimes apply to the slave period as well; an appendix (p. 176) gives the number of Barbados (and other West Indian) immigrants to Trinidad from 1839 through the first six months of 1841.

MELIORA

Letters on the labouring population of Barbadoes. With a preface by Meliora.

London, 1858. *48 pp.*   [BL, CU]

The author has not been identified. The preface is dated Barbados, December 10, 1857, and the letters were originally addressed to the editor of the *Liberal* newspaper and published in it. An apparent plantation owner (though it is hard to tell if he is Barbadian or English) who writes from a reformist perspective on the way in which the black "peasantry" of Barbados should be treated. His general emphasis is that employers have a greater responsibility to their laborers than merely paying their wages; they also have responsibility for their moral and material welfare. Focusing on the "most fertile sources of degredation and suffering to our people," that is, housing, infant care and suffering, the lack "of sound Christian education," and the the neglect of the sick and aged, he provides details on such topics as Barbados's educational and medical systems, religious instruction, family and marriage, housing, treatment of sick and elderly, and the juvenile reformatory at Boarded Hall. Although not an especially rich source on such topics, many observations in this work would also apply to the later years of the slave period.

SHREWSBURY, JOHN V. B.
Memorials of the Rev. William J. Shrewsbury.
London, 1868. *528 pp.*   [BL]
Annotated in JSH-71, but the title is erroneously given as *Memorials of W. J. Shrewsbury.*

LEE, ROBERT E. (Ed.)
Memoirs of the War In the Southern Department of the United States. By Henry Lee.
New York, 1870. 3rd ed. *620 pp.*   [SIU]
General Henry Lee, otherwise known as "Light-Horse Harry," was a prominent officer in the American Revolution, a confidant of George Washington, a one-time governor of Virginia, and a member of congress from that state. In 1813, primarily for health reasons, he went to the West Indies although the United States was then at war with Britain. Assisted by President James Madison and Secretary of State James Monroe, Lee departed the United States in early May 1813 and went to Barbados; he lived there for about six months, until around January 1814, and ultimately spent about five years in various Caribbean islands.

The *Memoirs* per se contain no materials on Barbados, but the editor, the famous Confederate general and one of Henry Lee's sons, provides biographical materials on his father (pp. 11-79), including a few items pertaining to the former's residence in Barbados. (For other details on Henry Lee and his residence in Barbados, see Noel Gerson, *Light-Horse Harry: A Biography of Washington's Great Cavalryman, General Henry Lee* [New York, 1966], pp. 239-41;

Charles Royster, *Light-Horse Harry Lee* [New York, 1981], pp. 232-34, 238-39). Henry wrote a number of letters from the West Indies and Barbados (*Memoirs*, p. iii), but only a few have been identified, and they are scattered among several repositories, including, for example, the LC, NYHS, NYPL, and the Virginia Historical Society (see chapter 3, United States). None of these letters was personally examined, and in each case the repository in question may have more items written by Lee during his sojourn in Barbados. One of Lee's letters to President James Madison, dated Barbados, August 24, 1813 (see chapter 3, LC), is printed in the *Memoirs* (pp. 54-55); it briefly deals with personal matters, and notes that Lee is sending Madison a bottle of madeira and a green turtle, "the largest I can procure" (see also, Gerson, *Light-Horse Harry*, p. 240).

In addition, several letters between Henry Lee and Barbados's Governor George Beckwith, written while the former resided in Barbados, focussing on the war between the United States and Britain, are published in the *American Historical Review* 32, 1927, 284-92; the originals are in the PRO (CO 28/82).

STUART, WILLIAM KIER
Reminiscences of a soldier.
London, 1874. 2 vols.   [BL, NYPL]
As a young man, Stuart was in Barbados sometime between 1829 and 1830; his autobiography contains comments on the island's Jewish population, cockfighting, crab collecting, and the British military in Barbados, including the romantic relationship between an officer and woman who was a "native of Cuba, but of European parents" (vol. 1, pp. 97-123, 236-239).

PHILLIMORE, AUGUSTUS
The life of Admiral of the Fleet Sir William Parker . . . from 1781 to 1866.
London, 1876. 3 vols.   [NYPL]
This naval biography contains several brief references to Barbados (see index in vol. 3) where Parker, who had sometimes sailed under the command of Lord Nelson, landed on a few occasions during the Napoleonic wars. In a letter Parker wrote his father from Barbados in 1805 (pp. 291-95), he briefly comments on Lord Nelson and British naval strength on the island.

EVELYN, JOHN
Diary of John Evelyn . . . edited from the original mss.
London, 1879. 4 vols.   [SIU]
Evelyn apparently never visited Barbados, but his well-known seventeenth-century diary contains a few very brief references to the island, including a comment on a conversation with Governor Willoughby in 1662, mention of some French prisoners in 1665 who wanted to go to Barbados, and notice of the 1692 slave plot "to murder all their masters, discovered by overhearing a discourse of two of the slaves" (vol. 2, pp. 147, 184; vol. 3, pp. 106-7). Volume 3 (pp. 402-6) contains a lengthy letter, written in 1681, to William London in Barbados, referring to a variety of fruits and vegetables alien to England; the letter contains a few specific references to Barbados plant life. The volumes were edited by William Bray.

[SHILSTONE, E. M.]
"Barbadians who qualified as doctors of medicine at Edinburgh up to 1845."
JBMHS, 28, 1961, 149-51.
Taken from an 1846 publication in Latin. Listed are the names, years of graduation, and short latin titles of their theses. Some of the persons on this list are mentioned in JSH-71; others include J. G. Bascom (1833), J. Bush (1829), W. Clarke (1831), J. H. Culling (1809), F. Goding (1832), Thomas Pollard Pierce (1792), and W. C. Trotman (1834).

STEELE, RICHARD
The Spectator.
Oxford, 1965. 5 vols.   [SIU]
Edited by Donald F. Bond. Aside from Steele's account of Inkle and Yarico (vol. 1, pp. 49 ff; see also JSH-71, p. 21), this famous eighteenth-century literary magazine, edited by Steele and J. Addison, contains several minor references to Barbados (see index, vol. 5), including the comment "The island of Barbadoes (a shrewd people) manage all their appeals to Great Britain by a skillful distribution of citron-water [a type of brandy] among the whisperers about men in power" (vol. 3, p. 479).

PRIDMORE, F.
The coins of the British Commonwealth of nations. Part 3, West Indies.
London, 1965. *364 pp.*   [LC, SIU]

The most complete discussion available of Barbadian coinage (pp. 76-79, 82-89) which photographically reproduces some of the coins and tokens used on the island during the eighteenth century and first half of the nineteenth.

LABAREE, LEONARD WOODS (Ed.)
Royal instructions to the British colonial governors, 1670-1776.
New York, 1967. 2 vols.   [SIU, URB]
Originally published in 1935, these volumes contain full transcriptions from original documents and are organized topically, for example, The Assembly, Revenue and Finance, Currency, Justice, Military Affairs, External Relations, Trade Instructions. References to Barbados governors are scattered throughout the two volumes and relate to a variety of topics.

WYVILL, RICHARD A.
"Memoirs of an old army officer" [1814].
JBMHS, 35, 1975, 21-30.
Edited with an introduction and notes by Jerome S. Handler. Transcription of an 1814 manuscript describing Wyvill's visits to Barbados in 1796 and 1806-7; see JSH-71, pp. 176-77.

MCCUSKER, JOHN J.
Money and exchange in Europe and America, 1600-1775: A handbook.
Chapel Hill, 1978. *367 pp.*   [URB, SIU]
The Barbados section (pp. 239-45) contains a table (pp. 241-44), based on primary sources, which gives the "rate of exchange: Barbados on London, 1687-1775."

PUCKREIN, GARY
"The Carlisle Papers."
JBMHS, 35, 1978, 300-10.
Transcriptions of five documents written in the late 1620s. *See* chapter 3, United States, Huntington Library.

SANDERS, JOANNE MCCREE (Ed.)
Barbados records: wills and administrations, 1639-1680.
Marceline, Missouri, 1979. *555 pp.*
The first of three volumes compiled primarily for genealogical researchers (but serving other purposes as well). This useful volume contains hundreds of abstracts of wills which are located in the Barbados Department of Archives. The wills from

which the abstracts were compiled are largely copies that were made in the late nineteenth century and early twentieth; very few original early wills still exist in Barbados. The abstracts stress names, places, and dates, but occasionally provide other information such as manumissions of slaves or indentured servants or bequests they received. There is also a very detailed name index and an important introduction by Michael Chandler which places these abstracts in their archival context. *See also* Sanders 1980, 1981.

KENT, DAVID L. (Ed.)
Barbados and America.
Arlington, Virginia, 1980. *391 pp.*
                                    [LC, NL]
Hotten's classic transcription of the 1679/80 census (JSH-71, pp. 104, 149) only included five parishes; in this book, Kent transcribes all data on the remaining parishes and corrects Hotten's transcription errors. The 1715 census of Barbados's white population (JSH-71, p. 149) is also transcribed in its entirety. A detailed personal name index to the transcribed materials is provided, as are relevant introductory materials to each transcription.

SANDERS, JOANNE MCCREE (Ed.)
Barbados records: wills and administrations, 1681-1700.
Houston, Texas, 1980. *531 pp.*
See Sanders 1979, 1981.

[CAMPBELL, PETER]
Paintings and prints of Barbados in the Barbados Museum.
Bridgetown, 1981. *32 pp.*   [BMHS]
Detailed descriptions (and occasional reproductions) of about twenty-five items, mostly prints, from the eighteenth and early nineteenth centuries; some of the prints are also briefly noted in JSH-71, pp. 119-20.

SANDERS, JOANNE MCCREE (Ed.)
Barbados records: wills and administrations, 1701-1725.
Houston, Texas, 1981. *520 pp.*
See Sanders 1979, 1980.

BRANDOW, JAMES C. (Ed.)
Omitted chapters from Hotten's original list of persons of quality . . . and others who went . . . to the American plantations, 1600-1700.

Census returns, parish registers, and militia rolls from the Barbados census of 1679/80.
Baltimore, Maryland, 1982. *245 pp.* [LC]
Hotten did not completely transcribe materials from this well-known census (see JSH-71, pp. 104, 149). For the six parishes not transcribed by Hotten, Brandow provides the lists of landholders as well as the baptismal registers; also, the militia rolls of the island's eight regiments, and miscellaneous related materials.

SANDERS, JOANNE MCCREE (Ed.)
Barbados records: marriages, 1643-1800.
Houston, Texas, 1982. 2 vols.   [NYPL]
Transcribed from the parochial registers, located in the Barbados Department of Archives. Volume 1 contains marriages for St. Michael, Christ Church, St. James, and St. John; volume 2, St. Joseph, St.Lucy, St. Peter, St. Philip, and St. Thomas. Volume 2 also contains a 318-page name index to the contents of both volumes. St. Andrew and St. George are excluded because registers of marriages started after the period covered by these volumes.

ANDERSON, ALEXANDER
Alexander Anderson's Geography and History of St. Vincent, West Indies.
Arnold Arboretum, Harvard University, 1983. *98 pp.*   [H]
Transcribed and edited by Richard A. and Elizabeth S. Howard. Anderson, the second director of the St. Vincent botanical garden, visited Barbados during 1783 or 1784. Although his unpublished manuscript focuses on St. Vincent, Barbados is occasionally mentioned: its visibility from St. Vincent, geology (particularly the coral limestone from which is "formed the filtering stones, a branch of manufacture in the island"), the depletion of its woods by early settlers, and the frequent reinforcement of St. Vincent's early black population by runaways from neighboring islands, including Barbados (pp. 5, 33-34, 36, 44). (See also chapter 3, England, Linnean Society of London.)

BRANDOW, JAMES C. (Ed.)
Genealogies of Barbados families: from Caribbeana and the Journal of the Barbados Museum and Historical Society.
Baltimore, Maryland, 1983. *753 pp.*
                                    [NYPL]
Reprints a number of genealogical studies originally published in *JBMHS* and several

others that appeared in V. L. Oliver's *Caribbeana* (JSH-71); also several articles on Quakers. Accompanied by a sixty-page name index.

SANDERS, JOANNE MCCREE (Ed.)
Barbados records: baptisms, 1637-1800.
Baltimore, 1984. *808 pp.*   [NYPL]
From parish records held in the Barbados Department of Archives, the editor has "attempted to reproduce faithfully the records . . . and have included data I believe to be in error." Accompanied by a place name and 263-page personal name index.

SENHOUSE, JOSEPH
"Senhouse papers: The diary of Joseph Senhouse."
JBMHS, 37, 1985, 277-95; 37, 1986, 381-414; 38, 1988, 179-95.
Edited and brought into print by James C. Brandow, who provides background and very detailed notes to this manuscript (located in the Cumberland Record Office, Carlisle, England), and biographical information on Joseph Senhouse. The first published installment of the diary deals with Dominica (June-August, 1776), and contains a miscellany of information on that island, including details on the few remaining Carib Indians. Barbados is covered in the second and third installments, January 1, 1777-June 7, 1778. Although Senhouse lived in Barbados from 1776 to 1779, entries in the diary were not made daily. Most of the entries are brief. They include: references to his major social activities and the people he visited or with whom he dined; observations on the weather, especially its impact on agricultural conditions; work activities and sugar production at Grove plantation; comments on a variety subjects, for example, thefts at the Bridgetown Customs House, activities at Grove plantation, naval and merchant ship arrivals, poor whites, a free colored murder, punishment of slaves, and Codrington College. For a related manuscript by William Senhouse, Joseph's older brother, see JSH-71, p. 102 and chapter 3, England, Cumberland Record Office.

Newspapers

For a general background to Barbados newspapers during the slavery period and for problems in identifying and locating individual copies, see JSH-71, pp. 116-18, which also provides brief historical sketches of the various known papers. The following section only includes newspaper copies or newspapers *not* included in JSH-71.

Barbados Gazette

Founded in October 1731, the *Barbados Gazette* was the island's first newspaper. When JSH-71 was published, the earliest known preserved copy was April 14-18, 1733, but now Number V, Saturday, November 6, 1731 (BL; Burney 2896) is the earliest known copy of *any* Barbadian newspaper. One copy each of the issues for November 29-December 2, 1752 and December 13-16, 1752 also exist (HL, Stowe mss., STG, Box 25, items 57 and 58). A May 30, 1753 issue is in the BL (Burney 1052); the AAS has a photostat of this issue.

BAN holds issues from January 28, 1784, December 22, 1785, January 14, 18, and March 1, 1786; CU has a copy from March 21-25, 1789.

According to LJR (p. 392) the *Barbados Gazette* continued publication until "at least as late as February 18, 1792," but a March 16, 1797 copy of the paper (AAS), now extends the publication date until at least the latter date. For other extant copies of the *Barbados Gazette*, see JSH-71, pp. 116-17.

Barbados Globe and Demerara Advocate

A July 14, 1828 issue is located at the AAS (see also, JSH-71, p. 117).

Barbados Mercury (in 1805, changed to Barbados Mercury and Bridgetown Gazette)

The AAS holds issues from September 22, 1770, October 6, 1770, October 13, 1770, and September 2, 1775—the only known copies for these dates (JSH-71, p. 117). BAN has copies for November 1, 1783 and December 31, 1785; while a copy of the former exists in Barbados (JSH-71, p. 117), the latter is a unique copy for this date. The PRO has issues from December 8, 15, 22, 1781 (CO 28/59), and February 22, 1783 and December 2, 1786 (CO 28/60). The AAS has copies of the *Barbados Mercury and Bridgetown Gazette* for June 4-28, 1814, October 6, 1821, November 17, 1821, February 12-23, 1828, and March 22, 1831—the 1828 and 1831 issues appear to be the only known copies for these years. AAS also holds microfilm copies of the original issues, held in Barbados, from April 5, 1783 to December 11, 1784 and from January 8, 1805 through 1806; the American Philosophical Society (Philadelphia, Pa.) has microfilms of Barbados-held issues for April 5, 1783 to December 11, 1784 and July 21, 1787 to November 3, 1788.

Barbados Times

Not mentioned in JSH-71. RS (p. 125) writes: "A paper called 'The Barbados Times' appejared about 1814, of which we can furnish no particulars." In a short book published in Barbados (see chapter 1, Ryan 1816), Michael Ryan identifies himself as the "editor of the Times newspaper." Since Ryan became editor of the *Globe*, founded for Barbadians "who professed liberal principles," in October 1818 (RS, p. 405), the *Barbados Times*, of which there are no known copies, must have had a very short life. Ryan was appointed printer to the House of Assembly in 1821, and continued as owner of the *Barbados Globe* "for many years"; he died sometime before January, 1834 (*JBMHS* 4, 1937, 96; 14, 1946-47, 244; 17, 1950, 182).

The Western Intelligencer

Not mentioned in JSH-71. However, RS (p. 405), describes *The Western Intelligencer* as the "organ" of the Barbadian "aristocracy and their exalted notions" in 1819, and implies that it had started before October 1818. Michael Ryan, the *Barbados Globe* editor at this period, also refers to *The Western Intelligencer* in his contemporary book (see chapter 1, Ryan 1816). *The Western Intelligencer* probably had a short lifespan, but it is unknown when publication ceased. There are no known copies.

3

Manuscripts

ENGLAND

For a general introduction to Barbados manuscripts in England, see JSH-71 (pp. 126-27). The identification of additional relevant manuscripts has been greatly enhanced by the publication of *A Guide to Manuscript Sources for the History of Latin America and the Caribbean in the British Isles* (London: Oxford University Press, 1973), edited by Peter Walne [PW]. PW lists or describes many manuscripts and manuscript collections in England, Scotland, Wales, Northern Ireland, and the Republic of Ireland; its detailed index helps identify Barbadian and West Indian materials.

Some of the manuscripts in PW are described in JSH-71; others are noted in the following pages, but there remains a considerable number of manuscripts that have not been consulted. In particular, the researcher should consult PW for Barbados manuscripts in the following repositories (relevant pages in PW are given in parentheses): Bristol, Record Office (pp. 4, 5), Public Libraries (p. 5); Buckinghamshire, Sir Harry Verney (p. 14); Cambridge University, Magdalene College Library (pp. 15, 16), University Library (pp. 16, 20); Cornwall, G. G. Fortescue (p. 24); Derbyshire, Marquess of Lothian (p. 30); Gloucestershire, Duke of Beaufort (p. 34), Earl Bathurst (pp. 36, 37); Herefordshire, A. Powell, (p. 40); Hertfordshire, Record Office (p. 43); Lancashire, Record Office (p. 50); Lincolnshire, Archives Office (p. 54), Duke of Rutland (pp. 52-53); Liverpool, Record Office (pp. 45, 46; cf. JSH-71, p. 143); London, Guildhall Library (pp. 128, 132), Historical Manuscripts Commission (pp. 132-34), House of Lords, Record Office (p.

142), West India Committee (p. 520; cf. JSH-71, pp. 159-60); Manchester, John Rylands Library (p. 50); Northamptonshire, Duke of Buccleugh and Queensbury (p. 291); Oxfordshire, Duke of Marlborough, Blenheim Palace (p. 295), Lieut.-Col. James Hanbury (p. 337); Staffordshire, County Record Office (p. 342), William Salt Library (p. 343); Sussex, Lord Egremont (p. 351); Warwickshire, Earl of Denbigh (p. 353); Wiltshire, Marquess of Bath (p. 355); Yorkshire, County Record Office (p. 357), Central Library, Sheffield (p. 364).

Materials identified as West Indies in the PW index (pp. 577-79) will probably also contain Barbadian materials.

John W. Raimo, ed., *A Guide to manuscripts relating to America in Great Britain and Ireland: A revision of the guide edited in 1961 by B. R. Crick and Miriam Alman* (Westport, Conn., 1979; see JSH-71, p. 127 for reference to Crick and Alman) contains some materials that are mentioned in JSH-71 and PW and some that are not mentioned in either; the latter are noted below.

Finally, it should be emphasized that manuscripts mentioned in the following pages are not included in JSH-71, unless otherwise indicated.

British Library
London

The BL's Manuscript Division contains a number of manuscripts relating to early Barbados history among the Additional, Egerton, Harley, King's, Sloane, and Stowe collections; these are described in JSH-71 (pp. 129-37). PW lists the following

Fig. 1. Seventeenth-century manuscript map of Barbados from the British Library.

Additional manuscripts (mostly from the eighteenth century) which are not listed in JSH-71 and were not consulted: 4157, *fol. 172;* 14272; 21947, *fols. 47, 57, 159;* 35616, *fol. 9;* 35584, *fol. 324;* 35585, *fol. 89;* 35908, *fol. 287;* 36128, *fol. 64;* 38197, *fol. 32;* 38203, *fol. 324;* 38206, *fol. 84;* 38304, *fol. 107b;* 38219, *fol. 237;* 38222, *fol. 292;* 38227, *fol. 146;* 38228, *fol. 347;* 38229, *fol. 281;* 38310, *fol. 112;* 38329, *fols. 55, 82;* 38334, *fol. 187;* 38335, *fol. 278;* 38352, *fol. 193;* 38257, *fol. 335;* 38368, *fols. 275, 277;* 39854; 40374, *fol. 235;* 41738; 41739; 49185.

Additional manuscripts 5414, *fol. 15.* (originally Sloane *3243*). A map that is briefly mentioned in JSH-71 (p. 137), and has since been examined (Figure 1). Undated, but clearly of the seventeenth century, the mapmaker is unidentified. The handpainted map shows about 65 features, mainly along the coastal areas, including plantations, mills, towns, forts, churches, bays and coves, and rivers. This map is very similar to one in Sloane 2441 (*fols.* 2-3; see JSH-71, p. 135), also undated with an unidentified maker (Frontispiece). The Sloane map accompanied a 1683/84 account of Barbados sent by Governor Dutton to England (JSH-71, p. 135). Although the maps resemble one another greatly in content, scale and size, lettering, coloring, and various cartographic details (and probably were done by the same person), they are not replicas; there are occasional minor variations in spelling and abbreviations employed, as well as some differences in artwork. Photographic prints of Additional 5414 and Sloane 2441 are available from the BL, negatives 23938 and 33967, respectively. In general outline and some major cartographic details, both maps also resemble Ogilby's map, published in 1670 (see T. Campbell, *The Printed Maps of Barbados,* Map Collectors' Circle, London, 1965, Plate II, no. 3; see also, JSH-71, p. 8), but both Sloane 2441 and Additional 5414 identify more individual plantations and other geographical features.

In July 1986, I examined the Manuscript Division's catalog volumes of Additional and Egerton manuscripts for materials acquired by the BL between 1971 and 1985; these are the only two collections which would contain newly acquired West Indian materials. The detailed table of contents of these catalogs yielded very few

West Indian materials and none gave the impression of dealing with Barbados.

PW lists the following Sloane manuscripts except for 4065; I personally examined a number of these:

49. "John Cox, his travels over land into the South Seas, from thence round the South part of America to Barbados and Antigua," *64 fols.* This was published as *Sharp's Journal* in 1684 (JSH-71). The ship sailed into Barbados waters in January 1681/82, but fearing capture did not land and went on to Antigua; no information is given on Barbados. A copy of this manuscript is at the Magdalene College Library, Cambridge University (MS. 2349); another is at the National Maritime Museum, Greenwich (GOS/4).

1426, fols. 78-105. "Edward Maynard, various journals of his voyages between England and America, 1667-71." Contains at least one voyage to Barbados; the "journal" is a ship's log recording wind and weather conditions during the voyage.

2903, fols. 4, 30. PW lists these as "papers concerning Barbados and the Bermudas," but the folio pages cited contain no Barbados materials, an apparent error in PW.

4065, fols. 164-65. Not listed in PW. Letter from Thomas Walduck to James Petiver, London, May 20, 1714. A discussion of the Barbados climate and rainfall, the problems of growing various types of plants on the island, and experiments in growing vegetables while Captain Walduck had been stationed at Rupert's fort where "in the late warrs" he was "oblig'd to keep guard ... for severall years." Captain Walduck wrote a much better known account of Barbados in another series of letters to Petiver, described in JSH-71 (p. 135), which erroneously identifies him as J. Walduck.

The following Sloane manuscripts were consulted but contain no materials on Barbados: 179B, 978; the following were not consulted but may contain Barbados materials: 3308, 4043.

Buckinghamshire Record Office
County Hall, Aylesbury

In a review of JSH-71, the late Professor Neville Hall reports that the "Earl of Buckinghamshire manuscript collection contains the correspondence of Lord Hobart, Secretary of State for War and the

Colonies in the Addington Ministry, 1801-1804. Bundles A, B, P, R and Y contain some useful correspondence between Hobart and Addington, and several letters to governors and others which bear on Barbados" (*Caribbean Studies*, 14, 1975, 184). See also PW (pp. 8-9) for a calendar of letters pertinent to Barbados in the Hobart papers.

Cornwall County Record Office
County Hall, Truro

Raimo (p. 20) identifies a manuscript not in JSH-71 or PW: "Letter from Paschow Morshead to his mother describing visit to Barbados, New England, and Virginia, 1647" (DD. CN. 3478). A photocopy of this letter was obtained from the Cornwall County Record Office. A very short letter, it was written from Barbados on May 25, 1674. However, it contains no descriptions of visits to, or information on, the places mentioned by Raimo; rather it is a personal letter, dealing with the writer's current position in life and sundry family matters.

Cumberland Record Office
Carlisle

The Senhouse manuscripts contain "miscellaneous accounts and papers relating to the Senhouse family and its estates in Barbados and Dominica, 1771-1777" (PW, pp. 27-28). They include the diary of Joseph Senhouse, 1776-1778 (see chapter 1, Senhouse, Joseph, 1985, 1986, 1988), and an autobiographical account, written around 1791, by William Senhouse (Joseph's older brother) of his years in Barbados (JSH-71, p. 102; see also, below, Rhodes House Library). The Londsdale manuscripts include Barbados Council minutes, 1711-20, and "accounts, correspondence, and papers relating to the plantations of the Londsdale family in Barbados, 1670-1737" (PW, p. 28).

Customs and Excise
Mark Lane, London

Plantation Department Records. Customs 34/233-258. Twenty-six volumes (out of 297) relate to Barbados, 1797-1854. PW (p. 125) reports that "the intracies of

the administrative arrangements relating to the collection of customs duties in the United Kingdom" is effectively treated in B. R. Crick and Miriam Alman (*A guide to manuscripts relating to America in Great Britain and Ireland*, Oxford University Press, 1961, pp. 188-92); Raimo also (pp. 86-88) gives a lengthy introduction to the records of Customs, including those housed in the PRO.

Gloucestershire Records Office
Shire Hall, Gloucester

A musical transcription of a slave work song in the Gloucester Records Office is mentioned in JSH-71 (pp. 139-40), but Raimo (p. 34) provides information on other records not in JSH-71 or PW. GBR 1456/1576; 1457/1577. Two registers of recognizances, 1643-52: "The majority of the bonds relate to ships' cargoes, and give details of ships, tonnage, and shipping routes from Bristol and Ireland to Virginia, Barbados and St. Christopher . . . . Both volumes have a personal names index." GBR 1458A/1583, pp. 371-78. Apprenticeship register, 1645-59. "Apprenticeship bonds of men and women contracting to serve as indentured labour in Barbados and Virginia, 1659-1660."

Linnean Society of London
Burlington House, Piccadilly, London

The library of the Linnean Society contains the papers of Alexander Anderson, the second director of the St. Vincent Botanical Garden (see chapter 1, Alexander Anderson, 1983), who visited Barbados in 1783 or 1784. Among the Anderson papers, which were examined in July 1986, two major items pertain to the island:

"Barbados," an undated manuscript (MS. 610) of eleven and one-half letter-size pages located in a drawer with Anderson's other papers. Based on Anderson's observations, this manuscript is one of several similar descriptive pieces he wrote of other West Indian territories he visited. The Barbados account focuses on natural history and describes the island's physical geography (including its ravines and gulleys), topography, soils, denudation of indigenous woodlands and forests, the

Scotland District and its unique geological features (including occasional references to water supplies and pottery), springs and rivers, caves (including the Animal Flower Cave), monkeys ("so numerous are they now in the gullys that they are the greatest plague the planters have"), climate and weather conditions, and diseases. The account, which includes occasional references to Griffith Hughes's work (1750; JSH-71, p. 34), with Anderson's supporting or contradictory comments and observations, ends rather abruptly, suggesting that it was intended to be a longer work that was never finished.

"An Account of the Island of Barbadoes" is located in Drawer 5a which contains manuscripts submitted to the meetings of the Society for Promoting Natural History in London. This account of Barbados by Anderson was read (in absentia?) before the Society on March 28, 1785, and was probably written not long before. The account is in a small bound notebook, but not in Anderson's hand; it appears to be a contemporary copy. In any event, it is Anderson's account and is based on his observations in Barbados. The account primarily concerns Barbados's geological origins, although "how this island was formed into two parts so very different from one another may be a question not easy of solution." In addressing this issue, discussion ranges over Barbados's topography and geology in greater detail than in the manuscript described above. There are observations on the island's vegetation and plant life, food crops, soil, rainfall and droughts (and their effects on vegetation), elevations, "gulleys" and caves, landscape and views, and springs. A detailed description of the Scotland District includes comments on its natural features and attractive views, "Barbados tar" and its local uses, Chalky Mount, and pottery. The island's plant life is extensively discussed, and a list of "the plants which I have not seen in the other islands" is given in their Latin names. Although there is some slight overlap between this account and the above-mentioned undated one, the two are substantially different—one is not merely a paraphrase of the other.

The Ellis manuscripts in the Linnean Society contain a letter from Alexander Bruce to John Ellis, July 17, 1759, "sending productions of Barbados by a friend." This is mentioned in the society's printed calendar of the Ellis manuscripts (London, 1948), but was not consulted.

National Maritime Museum
Greenwich, London

The National Maritime Museum is briefly mentioned in JSH-71, but none of its Barbados manuscripts are listed. However, I examined some Barbados materials in June, 1974, but there are undoubtedly more among various collections relating to the West Indies (see PW, pp. 154-67).

BRA/133,134. Captain Marsden, "Journal of Voyage to West Indies and of Service There, 1803-10." An army officer assigned to West Indian service, he arrived at Barbados (en route to Dominica) on December 26, 1803, but only stayed a few days; his journal entry merely records his coming ashore and taking "quarters at Nancy Clarks." On May 30, 1804, he returns to Barbados where he is now stationed. His journal entries are very brief and simply record his main daily activities, for example, where and with whom he dined, news about military affairs elsewhere, ship and fleet arrivals, and so forth. There are no descriptive passages or social commentary on Barbados, although occasionally one gets a glimpse of military life on the island. Marsden left Barbados permanently on February 7, 1805.

GOS/4. See above, British Library, Sloane manuscripts 49.

THO/2b. Sir Charles Thompson, "Letters and Order Books Whilst on West Indian Station, 1772-8." Contains official orders, occasionally given to or from Barbados; of interest for naval matters.

According to PW (p. 164), The Phillipps Collection includes "instructions to prize commissioners in Barbados from Admiral Sir William Penn and General Robert Venables, 1654."

National Westminister Bank
41 Lothbury, London

The bank is the repository for "Charles Cave's Letter Book, 1815-1836." In 1822, Cave became the owner of one of Barbados's better-known plantations, variously called St. Nicholas Abbey, Nicholas Abbey, or St. Nicholas; he was the great-great-grandfather of the plantation's current owner, Lt. Colonel Stephen F. Cave. The letter book only contains summaries (not copies) of about four hundred letters that Cave wrote from England, Barbados, and America; most were written from England to Barbados, although in the earlier years a number were written from Barbados. They are addressed to various merchant firms, plantation managers, friends, family members, and treat a variety of family and business matters; the latter relate to the running of the plantation (he was an absentee owner), and its agricultural production; also there are a few materials on the 1816 slave revolt. The writing is very small and cramped and often very difficult to read, but a handwritten calendar, prepared by Miss J.M.R. Campbell, the Westminister Bank's archivist, facilitates reading the letter book. A photo copy of the book is owned by Colonel Cave at St. Nicholas; I consulted this copy in March, 1977.

Oxford University
Bodleian Library

Some of the Bodleian's relatively large collection of Barbados manuscripts are described in JSH-71, but they were not consulted, and information on them was derived from published sources. PW lists more manuscripts in several collections, some of which (as noted below) I consulted in July 1974. What is described here supplements items listed and described in JSH-71; thus, the researcher interested in Barbados manuscripts in the Bodleian, most of which date from the seventeenth century, should consult JSH-71 as well as PW.

Ashmolean Manuscripts. See JSH-71 (p. 145) or PW (p. 297).

Bankes Papers. Not in JSH-71. See PW (p. 310) for three 1639 items; two relating to Henry Hunckes as governor, and the third a "commission" to Henry Hawley to negotiate the ending of tobacco planting in Barbados.

Clarendon Manuscripts. About thirty-two items, dating between 1647 and 1686. JSH-71 merely gives a brief general summary of some of these manuscripts, but PW (pp. 299-305) provides a more complete list with more details. The manuscripts include letters and other documents from or about such persons as Samuel Barwick, Richard Dutton, Francis Willoughby, Henry Willoughby, William Willoughby, Thomas Modyford, Humphrey Walrond, and D'Estrades. Topics dealt with include Cavalier-Roundhead antagonisms, military and naval issues in Barbados and the Leewards (particularly Montserrat and Nevis), Barbados's defenses, attack on St. Kitts, sugar tax on property, machinery in sugar mills, trade with the Dutch, war with the Dutch and French, De Ruyter's attack on Barbados, the governor's administrative problems, taxation, transporting persons to Barbados, an indictment against John Jennings for "using seditious words against the Governor," Willoughby's death, complaints against Governor Dutton, and a list of Barbados Council members. The following manuscripts were consulted: 81, *fols. 129-30*; 84, *fols. 126-28*; 85, *fols. 264-65*; none contain materials on slavery.

Rawlinson Manuscripts. PW (pp. 311-26) describes about thirty-two items, mostly from the last half of the seventeenth century, with a few from the early eighteenth. Eight of these manuscripts are included in JSH-71 (pp. 145-46); however, JSH-71 also describes some items not included in PW, and it should be noted that a number of the West Indian items in PW may also contain materials relevant to Barbados. Materials listed in PW (which should be consulted for more details) treat such subjects as trade with Hamburg, Sweden, and other non-English nations, land ownership conflicts in Barbados, relations with Spain, relations with Oliver Cromwell, administrative appointments, Admiralty court proceedings, transportation of Scottish prisoners to Barbados, powers of governor, disputes with assembly, goods exported, list of seventy-four plants found in Barbados, Act relating to ecclesiastical court, ship's log, and copy of Codrington's will bequeathing his plantation to the Society for the Propagation of the Gospel. Persons mentioned include Thomas Chapman, Christopher Codrington, John Colleton, Benjamin Cryer, Beville Granville, George Hannay, Robert Harmsworth, George Lillington, Samuel Pepys, David Ramsey, Governor Searle, Michael Terril, and John Yeamans.

A couple of manuscripts mentioned by PW were searched in July 1974: "Letter from Colonel Brayne giving an account of his voyage to Barbados," December 1, 1656, a two-page letter with no descriptive materials of the island; and "letter of Marcellus Rivers to Major-General Browne complaining of unjust transportation of royalist supporters to Barbados," November-December 1658, which has been removed from the volume and could not be examined.

<u>Rawlinson A. 348</u>. [Henry Drax], "Instructions which I would have observed by Mr. Richard Harwood in the management of my plantation according to the articles of agreement between us which are here unto annexed" [ca. 1670-79]. This manuscript (hereafter referred to as Rawlinson ms.) is not mentioned in JSH-71, and was brought to my attention by Douglas Armstrong; he generously provided a photocopy of it as well as his uncorrected transcription. PW (p. 320) lists Rawlinson ms. (ascribing neither date nor author), but erroneously identifies it as pertaining to a Jamaican sugar plantation, undoubtedly relying on the Rawlinson ms. cover page (added by an unknown cataloger [?]); internal evidence, however, plainly shows that the manuscript relates to Barbados.

Of twenty-four closely written folio pages, Rawlinson ms. is unsigned and undated, but its grammar, style, and orthography are typically mid-to-late seventeenth century. In addition, several of its pages are in a contemporary hand different from most of the other pages, suggesting that the manuscript is a copy.

A valuable source for plantation operations at this early period, Rawlinson ms. ranges over a variety of topics (some very briefly), including: the duties and obligations of the manager; food production for his own table; plantation cattle and their care; sugar cultivation, grinding, boiling, and curing; rum manufacture and the transportation of sugar, rum and molasses to Bridgetown; white servants; construction and repair of plantation buildings and windmills; and bookeeping and inventory procedures. Also discussed are matters relating to slaves, such as medical care, preferred ethnic groups, food supplies, clothing and other allowances, specialized occupational roles, behavioral characteristics such as theft, suicide, drunkenness, the gang organization of labor, and discipline.

What is obviously a version of Rawlinson ms. was included in William Belgrove's *A Treatise Upon Husbandry* , published in 1755 (JSH-71). Belgrove identifies himself as a "regular bred, and long experienced planter of . . . Barbados." His book contains a section by Henry Drax, a wealthy and prominent Barbados planter, entitled "Instructions for the management of Drax Hall and the Irish Hope plantations . . ." (hereafter referred to as Belgrove-Drax or "Instructions"). According to Belgrove, the "Instructions" were "given many years ago," but Belgrove does not date them nor describe how he acquired them. The "Instructions" (which had not been published prior to 1755) were addressed to Archibald Johnson, Drax's manager while the manager addressed in the Rawlinson ms. was Richard Harwood. Nonetheless, the unidentified author of Rawlinson Ms. also owned Drax Hall and Hope plantations, and very clearly the Rawlinson ms. and Belgrove-Drax are very closely related to one another.

A systematic comparison of both items shows that they are very similar, at times almost identical, in content, and this similarity almost extends over the entirety of both works; that is, the similarity is not limited to an occasional sentence or paragraph. Roughly the same amount of the Belgrove-Drax materials is included in the Rawlinson ms. and visa versa. Each item, however, contains materials that are absent from the other, although such materials constitute a minority of each.

Despite their great similarity in content, a major difference between Belgrove-Drax and the Rawlinson ms. is the manner in which the content is organized. Belgrove-Drax consists of seventy-six consecutively numbered "Instructions," ranging from a sentence or two to long paragraphs, sometimes running several pages. Most (sixty-three out of seventy-six) of the Belgrove-Drax "Instructions" are also in the Rawlinson ms. Yet the latter (which does not contain a numerical ordering) has them arranged in a very different sequence, and the "Instructions" are scattered about, rarely following the Belgrove-Drax sequence; here the two items bear little resemblance to each other.

Another difference is in the personal names mentioned in each item. Belgrove-Drax only mentions Henry Drax as the author (and plantation owner) and

Archibald Johnson, the plantation manager to whom the "Instructions" are addressed. The Rawlinson ms. is addressed to Richard Harwood, the plantation manager (Archibald Johnson is not mentioned in the Rawlinson ms.); other names include John Codrington (identified in the Rawlinson ms. as the author's cousin and apparently his agent when absent from the island), James Abel (a doctor administering to the plantations' slaves), and Christopher Lord (a plantation employee, perhaps the head overseer).

Of these names, additional information could be obtained only on John Codrington, but this information assists in establishing Henry Drax as the author of the Rawlinson ms., as well as the approximate date when the manuscript was written. The Codrington and Drax families, both prominent planter families, became related through marriage after the mid-seventeenth century. Codrington died in late 1686 or early 1687, and Henry Drax died in London in September 1682 (*JBMHS* 11, 1944, 106-8; 12, 1945, 72-73; 21, 1953, 21, 22-25; 26, 1959, 54-55).

Thus, although the author of the Rawlinson ms. is not given in the manuscript itself, several lines of evidence plainly indicate that he was Henry Drax: 1) the great similarity between the 1755 Belgrove-Drax and the Rawlinson ms. indicates that Henry Drax, the known author of the former, was also the author of the latter; 2) in his book, Belgrove himself notes that the "Instructions" were "given many years ago" by Henry Drax; 3) the unidentified Rawlinson ms. author mentions that he owns Drax Hall and the Hope plantations; Henry Drax is known to have owned these adjoining plantations (see *JBMHS*, 21, 1953, 22-25); 4) the unidentified Rawlinson ms. author notes that his cousin and friend is John Codrington; Codrington is established as the cousin of Henry Drax in other sources and is mentioned in Drax's will.

Although the Rawlinson ms. is undated, available evidence suggests a fairly narrow time period within which it was probably written. As noted above, Henry Drax died in London in 1682; thus, the manuscript was written before this date. The Rawlinson ms. (p.6) mentions that Drax intends sending his Barbados manager white servants "immediately after my arrival in England," suggesting that his "Instructions" were drafted before he left Barbados. Although Drax apparently made trips to England in the early 1670s, his last trip seems to have been made on April 22, 1679; he evidently remained in England until his death (*JBMHS*, 1, 1934, 161 ; *Calendar of State Papers, Colonial Series, America and West Indies, 1669-74*, p. 172; *1677-80*, pp. 588, 1513; *1681-85*, p. 540).

Nathaniel Lucas, an early nineteenth-century Barbadian historian who had access to many documents that no longer exist, ascribed a 1670 date to the Belgrove-Drax publication: the item was written, Lucas writes, "at the time when the fertility of the soil had abated; and it is extremely curious . . . that nearly a century afterwards, Belgrave [*sic*] should have written his Treatise . . . , as adopted to these very identical estates [Drax Hall and Hope]; it is . . . a real curiosity—1670 and 1755" (*JBMHS*, 1953, 21, 25). Lucas provides no evidence for his 1670 date and does not suggest how Belgrove obtained Drax's "Instructions" for publication; moreover, as noted above, Belgrove also does not report how he obtained the "Instructions." In any case, it seems likely that Belgrove's 1755 publication of Drax's "Instructions" was adopted from a Drax manuscript. There may have been several versions of this manuscript (as indicated earlier, for example, the Rawlinson ms. appears to be a contemporary copy) and Belgrove undoubtedly modified the one that came into his hands, at the minimum converting it into the style, grammar, and spelling of the mid-eighteenth century. In summary, then, the Rawlinson ms. is probably a copy, albeit a contemporary copy, of a manuscript that Henry Drax wrote sometime between 1670 and 1679, the former date perhaps just prior to an early trip to England, the latter prior to what appears to have been his last trip to the "mother country."

Found with the Drax manuscript in Rawlinson A. 348 are three other items, none of which appear to be related to the Drax manuscript and which may have been inadvertently included in Rawlinson A. 348: 1) a three-page contemporary copy of the Council minutes of St. Jago, Jamaica, February 10, 1689/90; 2) a 1690 "memorandum" of a few lines, noting a financial loan and payments on it; the name and place of the lender is not given;

3) "inventory of my owne linen and wearing cloths taken Aprill 1693," a brief list of items; neither the owner nor the place is indicated.

Tanner Manuscripts. JSH-71 (pp. 146-47) contains some information on Barbados manuscripts that is not available in PW; on the other hand, PW (p. 296) lists some manuscripts not in JSH-71, and provides a little more precise information on some others that are listed. Most Tanner manuscripts are from 1651, although a few are from later in the seventeenth century. They deal with the state of the church, royalist complaints about Barbados's "oppressive government," and surrender to forces of parliament. Persons mentioned include Jonathan Atkins, George Ayscue, Richard Dutton, and Francis Willoughby. One of the manuscripts listed in PW (p. 296) was consulted: "A letter from Sir George Ayscue in Barbados to the Council of State, on the condition of the island," October 31, 1651; it deals with military and naval matters, not civil affairs.

Other Bodleian Collections. Several Barbados manuscripts not included in JSH-71 are described in PW (see pages 323-25 for more details): entries made in the Barbados Custom House, 1664-65 (see also, below, Hispanic Society of America); instructions from a slaving company to its captain sailing from Bristol to West Africa and Barbados, 1792; letter concerning the introduction of paper money, 1723; "A short view of the present state of Barbados," concerning paper money, n.d.; appeal for clergy for Barbados, 1827; notes by Dr. Thomas Smith, includes documents about Barbados copied from the papers of Governor Richard Dutton, 1680-1700.

The only item in this group (PW, p. 324) that was personally consulted (in July 1974) was: "Two narratives by female slaves at Barbados, written down there by John Ford, 1799" (MS. Eng. misc. b. 4, *fols. 50-51*). Two foolscap pages, with writing on each side, containing accounts "related to the writer by an Old African female slave named Sibell . . . [and] an old female slave named Ashy of the Fantee tribe." The transcriber has not been identified, but these brief accounts are supposed to be literal transcriptions of the slave dialect; there is no indication of the conditions under which the narratives were related and the transcriptions made. If they are legitimate, they offer interesting and rare materials for the study of the Barbadian creole language as well as unusual documents in which African-born slaves relate their experiences before they came to Barbados. In her narrative, Sibell tells something of her family life in Africa, how she was captured and sold as a slave, her reactions to seeing white people and the sea for the first time ("me nebber see de white people before, me nebber see de great ships pon de water before, me nebber hear de waves before which me frighten so muchee dat me thought me would die"), and how various countrywomen of hers on the ship were sold "and me no savvy where now"; at this, the narrative abruptly ends when Sibell "burst into tears and could say no more."

Ashy's account is shorter and contrasts Africa with Barbados: "Ah! Massah dis country here dat you call Barbadus, um no good, um no good"; she describes how easy it is to bring rain in Africa through the efforts of a conjurer and by sacrificing a sheep, and how if servants of some important man run away and return after a long time, they are not punished as they are in Barbados.

Oxford University
Rhodes House Library

The Rhodes House Library holdings were very briefly and generally noted in JSH-71, but no details were given. The holdings in the library are listed in Louis B. Frewer, *Manuscript Collections (excluding Africana) in Rhodes House Library Oxford* (Bodleian Library, 1970): some not noted in Frewer are described in PW. Some of the Rhodes House manuscripts were examined in July 1974.

MSS. Brit. Emp. s. 20. "Letters and reports received by the Secretary and Trustees of the Mico Charity, bound into volumes, from the superintendents and teachers in the schools established by the charity in the West Indies to educate former slaves and their children in the period of apprenticeship . . . 1835-1842"; the Barbados correspondence is in MSS. Brit. Emp. s. 20, E. 1/3 (PW, p. 326).

MSS. Brit. Emp. s. 22. A miscellany of letters, reports, etc. dating from nineteenth and early twentieth centuries. Barbados manuscripts are in MSS. Brit.

Emp. s. 22, G. 54. This file folder contains about twenty-five items dating from the 1840s to the 1880s. The folder includes letters addressed to the British and Foreign Anti-Slavery Society; some of the early letters are from "colored" men such as C. Phipps and Samuel Prescod. About four 1840 letters from Prescod (to J. Sturge, J. H. Tredgold, and John Scoble) strenuously object to efforts by the Barbados government to curtail the emigration of laborers to British Guiana and Trinidad; some letters contain information on social, political, and economic conditions. There is also an undated (1840?) petition addressed to Lord Carnarvon, the Secretary of State for the Colonies, from "a representative committee for the coloured and black races of the inhabitants of the colony"; they request an extension of the franchise "as we are not represented in the legislative assembly," and other reform measures, including "the necessity of thinning the population by opening the way to a liberal emigration." The petition is accompanied by a list of the fourteen signatories, their occupations, and parishes of residence.

MSS. West Ind. r. 5, 6. Diary of William Senhouse (Barbados and Leeward Islands) copied and completed by Sir H. F. Senhouse, 1750-1800. 2 vols. (Frewer, no. 621). I am not sure how this item relates to that in the Cumberland Record Office (see this chapter, above).

MSS. West Ind. s. 16 (2) and MSS. West Ind. t. 3. Lucie Smith family. "Miscellaneous correspondence, certificates and papers of the Lucie Smith family of Barbados from 1698," and "pedigree of the Lucie Smith/McLaurin family" (Frewer, nos. 589, 590; cf. PW, p. 328); contains materials of genealogical interest.

MSS. West Ind. s. 4, fols. 118-26. Letter from Sir Henry Warde, Governor of Barbados to Sir William Henry Clinton, dated Barbados, October 10, 1821 (Frewer, no. 636). This long and detailed letter is marked confidential. The governor is generally distressed at conditions on the island, the state of its defenses, his inability to cope with conditions, the sickness of troops, and so forth. He complains about his own limited finances and the cost of living, admits that "I cannot say that I very much fancy the black population here," discusses the murder of Mr. Elcock by slaves, the slave laws, his views on teaching slaves to read ("they would not become better men but worse by reading"), and feels that "it would require very little to move the black population to play a second St. Domingo scene." This letter, as well as about twenty-one others from Warde to his friend Clinton (from a private collection now located in the library of the Barbados Museum), over the period 1821-1830, have been printed in *JBMHS*, 34, 1974, 198-208; 35, 1975, 51-59; 35, 1976, 120-37; editorial notes give background to the letters and biographical details on Warde and Clinton.

(B) MS. Sherard 477. "Account book of cargos shipped to Jamaica, Barbados, Antigua, St. Lucia and St. Kitts, 1782-1783" (Frewer, no. 637).

Public Record Office
London

Since publication of JSH-71, the Colonial Office papers, among other PRO collections, have been moved to the new PRO at Kew Gardens; although distant from central London, Kew Gardens is an impressive repository, superbly organized and efficiently run, with modern facilities and comfortable accommodations for readers. JSH-71 (pp. 147-52) makes some attempt to describe the massive PRO collections, particularly the papers of the Colonial Office, and various published guides useful in approaching these collections; some Barbados manuscripts in the Colonial Office papers (CO 1, 28, 29, 30, 31, 33) and the Shaftesbury papers (PRO 30/24; cf. PW, pp. 250-51) were also described. (JSH-71, p. 149, lists Atkins, "Answers to 32 queries," July 4, 1676; the class number, inadvertently omitted in publication, is CO 1/37, *fol.* 67.)

PW (pp. 168-279) provides a great deal of background information on the major record groups and classes, for example, Chancery, Exchequer, High Court of Admiralty, State Paper Office, Admiralty, Colonial Office, Board of Customs and Excise, Board of Trade, Treasury, War Office; and occasionally specifically identifies Barbados manuscripts (see C 103/137, p. 171; C 105/27, 28, p. 172; C 110/31, p. 175; C 110/173, 175, p. 176; Navy Board, p. 194; Hospital Musters, p. 196; T 38, p. 261; WO 55, p. 276; WO 28, p. 278). See also Raimo (p. 88) for a description of the Board of Trade Series,

Custom House Accounts (<u>CO 390/6-11</u>), for tables of goods exported and imported by various colonies, including Barbados, 1677-1731. George and Carolyn Tyson briefly annotate manuscripts, mostly from the PRO, some of which relate to Barbados (*Preliminary report on manuscript materials in British archives relating to the American revolution in the West Indian islands*, St.Thomas, U. S. Virgin Islands, 1974, pp. 8-14).

University of London Library
Senate House, London

Two manuscript collections at the University of London Library, the William Hewitt Papers (<u>MS. 522</u>) and the very important Newton Estate Papers (<u>MS. 523</u>), dealing with Newton and Seawell plantations and comprising well over 1,000 documents, are described in JSH-71. In 1974, the University of London Library purchased an additional eighty-three documents, primarily dating from the 1680s and 1690s, relating to Newton, and providing useful information on legal and economic affairs (<u>MS. 523/1054-1702</u>). The whole body of Newton manuscripts (including those located at the University of London, the PRO, the Barbados Museum Library, and the Barbados Department of Archives) are described in great detail (with a brief history of Seawell and Newton and a description of the handlists available for their study) in Jerome S. Handler, "Sources for the Study of Preemancipation Sugar Plantations in Barbados: Manuscripts Relating to Newton and Seawell," *Caribbean Archives*, 5, 1976, 11-21.

Another Newton manuscript was brought to my attention in 1977 by Lt. Colonel Stephen Cave, the owner of Nicholas Abbey plantation, who possesses

the manuscript. It is a long letter from Thomas Horner in Barbados to Barbara Newton in London, January 17, 1687/88; Barbara was the widow of Samuel Newton, the original owner of the plantation. This is now the earliest known account of the state of the Newton plantation. Thomas Horner apparently was Barbara Newton's attorney and he was trying to collect debts owed her from various persons in Barbados; he also reports on her plantation, its financial condition, the debts and rents owed, the nature of the sugar crop to be produced, and gains from sugar manufacture. He reports he has "hired a refiner until you send one from England," suggests that Barbara Newton "would doe well to . . . send over some tradesmen, such as would be fitt for your service as taylor, smith or any other trade . . . with some ordinary servants because of the militia," notes a "great loss of negroes," but "we shall make good shift this year" with seven who were newly purchased. Richard Bates is the plantation manager; other persons mentioned include Messrs. Beale, Claypoole, Cryer, Gibbs, Hallet, Horstall, Johnson, and Sutton.

PW (p. 289) also records the following Barbados manuscripts in the University of London Library:

<u>MS. 279</u>. "Proposal by John Ashley, member of the Council of Barbados, for a capitation tax on sugar and salt to replace duties on the produce of West Indian plantations so that Great Britain may better compete with France, c. 1749."

<u>MS. 401</u>. "Documents relating to the 4 1/2 % duty levied in Barbados and the Leeward Islands, 1669-1682."

<u>MS. 407</u>. "Petition of creditors of Sir William Courten [*sic*] to compel merchants who have unlawfully repossessed Sir William of his plantations in Barbados to make redress to them, 13 September, 1671."

IRELAND AND SCOTLAND

JSH-71 (pp. 160-65) describes some manuscripts in Irish and Scottish repositories. PW records others in the following: <u>Belfast</u>, Public Record Office (pp. 435, 436); <u>Edinburgh</u>, National Register of Archives (pp. 395, 396),

University of Edinburgh Library (pp. 429, 431); <u>Glasgow</u>, City Archives (p. 382). JSH-71 describes Barbados manuscripts in the Scottish Record Office, Edinburgh; PW adds some others in the same repository (pp. 415, 428).

National Library of Scotland
Edinburgh

The Barbados holdings in the National Library of Scotland were not described in JSH-71, although subsequent to its publication relevant manuscripts were identified through PW (pp. 382-95); a few others were brought to my attention by Dr. Paul Kelly, Assistant Keeper of the Department of Manuscripts. Some of these manuscripts were personally examined and are described below; others are simply noted, and the researcher is referred to PW for details.

Cochrane Papers. MS. 2573, the printed catalog of the National Library, suggests this is chiefly the official correspondence, concerning Barbados and St. Vincent, of Sir Alexander Forrester Inglis Cochrane, consisting of letters addressed to him and copies and drafts of letters written by him, 1810-11. MS. 2577-2578, 2583-2589, private journal of Admiral Thomas Cochrane, twenty-eight volumes of small notebooks covering his service in Barbados and the West Indies, 1807-10, 1813, 1815, 1821-24. This was only skimmed but he was in Barbados at least as early as November 1807; the journal entries are brief and the handwriting is very cramped.

Houston Papers. Letters and accounts books of Alexander Houston and Company, regarding trade between Glasgow and West Indies, including Barbados, 1776-81 (see PW, p. 393).

Melville Papers. MS. 1083, Journal of J. Ker, Surgeon, Royal Navy, 1778-82. Ker left England on January 1, 1779, arriving at Barbados on February 9, 1779. The journal section on Barbados (pp. 23-24) contains a water colorsketch, the Scotland District as viewed from St. John's church. The journal entries barely cover two sides of one foolscap page, and are mainly jottings of the people he saw and with whom he stayed. Virtually nothing is said about Barbados per se other than a brief comment on the white women and their physical features. After visiting St. Lucia, Dominica, St. Kitts, etc., he returns to Barbados in August, 1779, but his month-long stay receives the same treatment in his journal as the earlier one. MS.1711, *fols. 75-77*, Barbados population totals, 1802, of whites, free coloreds, and slaves, by sex; the acreage of each parish; goods exported from the island, 1802; the annual number of slaves imported, exported, and taxed, 1788-1804; baptisms and funerals in St. Michael, November 30 1804-November 30, 1805.

Murray Papers. General orders of Sir Ralph Abercromby, 1796; various papers dealing with military matters, 1802-03; correspondence with Major Eckersley regarding ordnance affairs, 1829 (PW, p. 383).

Nisbet Papers. According to the printed catalog of the National Library MS. 5498, *fol. 33*, is a financial account concerning Barbados, 1790-91.

Stuart De Rothesay Papers. Relating to Lady Seaforth, 1802-4, 1812 (PW, p. 392).

Tweeddale Papers. Not listed in PW. The following information was provided by Paul Kelly (personal communication, November 13, 1975): " . . . some Barbadian material [in the] letters and papers (thirty-nine folios in total) of William Paterson, Suveyor-General of the Leeward Islands, in the Tweeddale papers, 1749, 1757, 1761-62. The material is addressed to the Marquess of Tweeddale under whom Paterson had served as Chief Clerk in the Scottish Department, 1742-7. Most of this material consists of essays or papers by Paterson expounding his views concerning the peace settlement, the 'Canada versus Guadeloupe' controversy, etc. . . ." A photocopy of this five-page letter (Acc. 4862, Box 9, F.1. b) was obtained: Written in Barbados, July 29, 1749, it briefly discusses family matters relating to the Marquess of Tweeddale, provides some autobiographical information on Paterson (who had been in the West Indies for about two years, principally residing in Barbados), and offers various comments on "these islands," where he finds "the same dull face of tranquility over the whole; all cane land, except small patches of very indifferent pasture." Brief observations are given on slave work patterns ("working no faster than needs must attend . . . the females, some of them boiling in the sun with infants hanging at their backs"), the white overseer, the planters ("whose conversation, . . . excepting a very few, . . . turns for the most part on windmills, cattlemills, canes, sugar boiling, distilling, cockfighting etc."), whites in the towns (who are "more polite and sociable"), the cost of living ("everything is excessive dear, and eatables so much the dearer"). In all, "there is nothing very captivating or bewitching" in the West Indies and were it not for his job and debts he "would not stay long in these most inconvenient and intollerable climates where, whatever a man gets, he most dearly earns." PW (p. 325) reports that the Bodleian Library has the "Papers of William Patterson, Surveyor-General of the Leeward Islands, 1761-2" (MS. North b. 6, *fols. 1-28*); these may contain some Barbados materials.

Yester Papers. Relating to John and William Brown, trading between Scotland and Barbados, ca. 1663-66 (PW, p. 392). Dr. Paul Kelly (personal communication, September 5, November 13, 1977) provides the following references: "the probate testament of Archibald Hay, St. George parish, Southwark, 1655, chiefly concerning the Spring plantation in Barbados, and property in Antigua, which he bequeaths to his nephew, Archibald Powrey" (Ch. 10868); letter of Thomas Finlay to John McFarlane, Barbados, 1736, "concerning slave troubles on Antigua" (MS. 6415, no. 71).

FRANCE

The Muséum d'Histoire Naturelle at Le Havre contains the "Sketchbooks of Charles Alexandre Lesueur, 1815-1837." The Le Havre-born Lesueur was a naturalist who went to the United States and ultimately spent about twenty-one years in America, particularly Philadelphia and the midwest. A major result of Lesueur's voyages was his production of about 1,400 to 1,500 drawings and watercolors of the places he visited. On his way to the United States, he passed through the West Indies and spent about four months traveling through the islands. Departing Falmouth on November 16, 1815 and accompanied by the American geologist William Maclure, Lesueur's first stop was Barbados; he stayed for two weeks, December 31, 1815 to January 13, 1816. He made a number of drawings of the island, and, apparently, recorded his observations in a separate small notebook.

JSH-71 (p. 167) gives a general description of Lesueur's Barbados drawings, but this was based on published sources and a brief letter from A. Maury, the Director of the Muséum d'Histoire. However, the Muséum d'Histoire was visited in July, 1974 and the Barbados drawings were examined. They are in two small notebooks (about 3 1/2 wide by 6-7 inches long) that contain Lesueur's other West Indian drawings. There are twenty-four sketches of Barbados (KEI, p. 78, basing his information on a letter from Maury, errs in saying there are only fourteen): all are in pencil, appear to be rapid sketches, and offer few details; some appear unfinished, perhaps to be completed at a later date under more leisurely conditions. The drawings are largely of scenery and geological formations, and very few are titled although some contain a descriptive word or phrase or two.

Drawing 1) Appears to be a coral formation. 2) Profile of island's elevation as approached from the sea. 3) Appears to show a black woman with a pail on her head (a very small drawing with little detail). 4) Duplicate of previous. 5) A grotto (probably the Animal Flower Cave in St. Lucy). 6) A scene of hills and houses (very vague in detail). 7) A sugar mill, plantation house, and cane field; one of the clearer drawings (Figure 2). 8) Unfinished drawing of a windmill. 9) Woods or a grove of trees. 10) Incomplete drawing of human figures, but difficult to decipher what/who they are. 11) Unfinished, a very rough sketch of an undecipherable subject. 12) Ditto. 13) Ditto. 14) Hill formations, perhaps the Scotland District; appears to show Hackelton's Cliff in the background. 15) A vague and generalized view of Bridgetown from some elevation. 16) Fishing boats (some with sails) in a bay with houses along the shoreline. This may be a view of Speightstown; limited detail, but one of the clearer drawings (Figure 3). 17) Vague drawing of scenery. 18) Grove of palm trees showing what is probably a slave house in the foreground and a couple of windmills in the background; another one of the clearer drawings (Figure 4). 19) Vague outlines of a geological formation. 20) General view of what

Fig. 2. Sugar plantation scene, Barbados, 1815-1816.

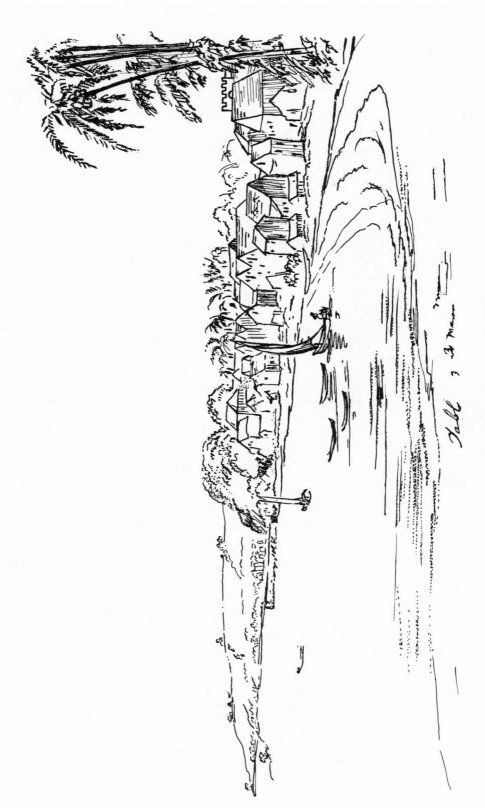

Fig. 3. Shoreline scene, Barbados, 1815-1816.

Fig. 4. Sugar mill, Barbados, 1815-1816.

appears to be Codrington College and surrounding plantation lands, showing outbuildings, windmill, etc. 21) Vague scene of what appears to be women washing in a pond or river; in the background, cane fields and some people with hoes. All lightly done and the detail is rather obscure. 22) Vague scene of island profile as it appears from the sea. 23) Very schematic and rapid sketch of Bridgetown from Carlisle Bay. 24) General view of Bridgetown and background hills from the sea ("Vue prise a notre depart de Barbados"), showing houses, a fort and a ship; the drawing indicates the location of the house in which he resided. For a list of drawings of other West Indian islands, see KEI, pp. 78-79. For details on the Lesueur drawings in general, see: W. G. Leland, "The Lesueur Collection of American Sketches in the Museum of Natural History at Havre" (*The Mississippi Valley Historical Review*, 10, 1923-24, 53-78); R. W. G. Vail, "The American Sketchbooks of a French Naturalist 1816-1837" (*Proceedings of the American Antiquarian Society*, 48, pt. I, 1938, 49-155); G. Chenard, "The American Sketchbooks of Charles-Alexandre Lesueur" (*Proceedings of the American Philosophical Society*, 93, 1949, 114-18); and, E. T. Hamy, *Les Voyages du Naturaliste Ch. Alex. Lesueur dans l'Amerique du Nord* (Paris, 1904).

After the Second World War, the American Philosophical Society, in cooperation with the Muséum d'Histoire Naturelle, microfilmed all of Lesueur's American sketchbooks. In 1956, a six-reel copy of the microfilm set was obtained by the Library of the Illinois Historical Survey at URB. Reel 3 contains Lesueur's West Indies sketches and notes. I examined this reel in 1981; it contains the Barbados drawings described in the preceding paragraph. Some of these drawing are faint, or even missing from the frame. Reel 5 has (in about a half dozen frames) Lesueur's account, in an often barely legible hand, of his preparations for his trip to America, the agreements he made with Maclure, what they hoped to accomplish, and the trip across the channel from France to England—this may be an excerpt from the first book of his journal.

In addition to the drawings, E. T. Hamy (p. 12) reports that "Lesueur's stay in the Lesser Antilles is recorded in his notes in a series of small notebooks, containing: Barbados, 14 pp.; Saint-Vincent, 14 pp.; Dominica, 9 pp. . . . etc. as well as a portfolio of pretty drawings preserved at the Museum of Le Havre" ("Le séjour de Lesueur dans les Petites-Antilles est représenté dans ses notes par une suite de petits cahiers, contenant: Barbados, 14 pp.; Saint-Vincent, 14 pp. . . etc. . . . plus un portefeuille de jolis dessins conservés au Museum du Havre"). Hamy's monograph is based on materials in the Muséum d'Histoire Naturelle in Paris (now the Muséum National d'Histoire Naturelle) and the Muséum d'Histoire Naturelle in Le Havre. The Muséum d'Histoire Naturelle does not have the "petits cahiers" or other Caribbean notebooks referred to by Hamy, and A. Maury did not know where they might be located. The Bibliotheque Centrale of the Muséum National has a number of Lesueur manuscripts, but Y. Laissus, one of the curators, briefly examined the collection and reported to me (personal communication, July 12, 1974) that he could not find the West Indies notebooks; he conjectured that the Muséum National did not possess them. It remains a mystery where these notebooks might be, although they may have been overlooked in the brief search conducted in the Muséum National.

The contents of the notebooks, however, are suggested in Hamy's monograph and his treatment of Lesueur's trip through the Caribbean islands; Barbados is dealt with on pages 12-15. The Barbados notebook appears to start with Lesueur's observations on the island's physical geography and cultural landscape as it is approached from the sea; their ship was greeted in the bay by small boats rowed by "jeunes mulatresses" who competed for travelers; they chose a residence owned by a Martiniquan woman whose French was fluent; soon after arrival, Maclure and Lesueur began exploring Bridgetown and the sea-shore, collecting a variety of fish, crustaceans, sea anemones and other zoological specimen. Taking a trip on horseback to Holetown, they were guided around by a Mr. Wint and learned that Bridgetown's growth had made Holetown almost deserted. Geological observations were made along the road from Bridgetown to Holetown, and other zoological specimen were collected along Holetown's beach. They continued their trip through Speightstown, commenting on the countryside, and visited Bourbon plantation; from there they traveled through St. Lucy to the Animal Flower Cave, "reputée une des curiosités de l'ile," which is described; they then returned to Bridgetown via St. Andrew. After a two-week stay at Barbados they left for St. Vincent.

UNITED STATES

Although JSH-71 (pp. 168-82) provides some information on Barbados manuscripts in the United States, the identification and location of such manuscripts has been considerably augmented and advanced by the publication of Kenneth E. Ingram's monumental *Manuscripts Relating to Commonwealth Caribbean Countries in United States and Canadian Repositories* (Barbados: Caribbean Universities Press, 1975) [KEI]. Ingram, the former head librarian of the University of the West Indies (Mona, Jamaica), has performed a considerable bibliographic service in compiling his detailed and carefully indexed work. This work includes a number of collections I had not personally consulted, but were nonetheless described in JSH-71, as well as a number of other collections of which I was unaware. KEI is an essential source for the location of Barbados (and West Indian) manuscripts in United States (and Canadian) repositories and was used to locate most of the repositories mentioned below.

The following descriptions include information on repositories that were not mentioned in JSH-71; with the exception of AAS, all are also mentioned in KEI. I try to avoid duplicating KEI and describe manuscripts or collections Ingram did not consult, minimally described, or did not describe at all. KEI, however, provides information on a variety of repositories that are not included in JSH-71 or in this *Supplement,* as well as on some repositories mentioned in JSH-71, but inadequately described (because they could not be visited); thus KEI should be consulted by anyone seriously searching for Barbados manuscripts.

KEI should be consulted for Barbados holdings in the following repositories, either not mentioned in JSH-71 or mentioned but for which KEI lists additional manuscripts (relevant KEI page numbers are in parentheses): Bancroft Library, University of California, Berkeley (pp. 2, 3, 4, 8); Essex Institute, Salem, Massachusetts (pp. 132-33; cf. JSH-71, p. 173); Folger Shakespeare Library, Washington, D. C. (p. 38); Harvard University, Baker Library (pp. 118-19, 121, 123); Henry Francis DuPont Winterthur Museum, Winterthur, Delaware (p. 37); Mariner Museum, Newport News, Virginia (pp. 299-301); Maryland Historical Society, Baltimore (p. 85; cf. JSH-71, p. 177); Massachusetts Archives, Boston (p. 105; cf. JSH-71, p. 101); Newport Historical Society, Newport, Rhode Island (pp. 268, 271); Rhode Island Historical Society, Providence (pp. 286, 290; cf. JSH-71, p. 180); South Carolina Archives Department, Columbia (p. 296).

American Antiquarian Society
Salisbury St., Worcester, Massachusetts

In June 1981, the AAS printed *Catalogue of the Manuscript Collections of the American Antiquarian Society* (Boston, 1979) was consulted; it contains only one listing under the heading "Barbados": Rose Family Papers, 1831-1906. These were not examined but they contain "Barbados notes," information for 1648-1731, collected from various sources in the nineteenth century by Frances Henry Lee for a genealogy of this family with West Indian and Worcester connections. The Rose Family Papers do not appear to contain any original manuscripts on Barbados.

Under the heading "West Indies," the *Catalogue* lists the Paine Family Papers, c. 1721-1918, and the Logbook Collection. The former do not appear to contain Barbados materials, while the latter contains: "*Success* (Brig), Captain Thaddeus MacCarty of Boston, 1670-1729. Log of 6 Trips to Jamaica, London, and Barbados, 26 December 1718 to 5 December 1719"; a conventional mariner's log, this has no information on Barbados per se. The only other log in this collection that seems to bear on the West Indies (the log of *Tyrannicide* , 18 June 1776 to 22 January 1777, Captain John Friske) contains no reference to Barbados.

American Philosophical Society
105 South Fifth St., Philadelphia, Pennsylvania

A microfilm copy was obtained of the 1671 manuscript by George Welch, "A journall of my voyage with ye sundry passages thereof as I travel'd into divers parts of the West Indies" (M S 917.29/W455). Welch, a Quaker, spent a day or so on Barbados, a few pages of his journal dealing with this visit. In many ways typical of contemporary Quaker writings, Welch only mentions the names of the people he saw and offers no descriptive information on Barbados. (For other Barbados manuscripts at the APS, see KEI, items 793, 794, 794a.)

Boston Public Library
Copley Square, Boston, Massachusetts

JSH-71 (pp. 169-72) describes a number of manuscripts in the Boston Public Library, but KEI (p. 102) adds an item (MS. U.1. 16) which contains a brief traveler's account of Barbados in the 1790s. In addition, the extremely valuable Colthurst Journal (JSH-71) has since been published with an important introduction by its editor, Woodville K. Marshall (*The Colthurst Journal* [New York: KTO Press, 1977]).

Colonial Williamsburg Foundation
Williamsburg, Virginia

In June 1988, the Curator of Special Collections notified me that the Colonial Williamsburg Foundation had two collections with Barbados materials. The William Blathwayt Papers "contain a wealth of information on Barbados for the late seventeenth and early eighteenth centuries." This collection is on microfilm (ten reels) and can be borrowed on interlibrary loan (reel number M-1524), two reels per request. None of these was personally examined, but KEI (p. 305)

reports that the collection contains 2,568 items in forty-one volumes. Volumes 29-35 deal with Barbados, 1675-1701, and contain "an extensive correspondence from governors and other officials addressed to Sir R. Southwell and William Blathwayt, with draft replies from Blathwayt, numbering some 385 items"; KEI names the letter writers in volumes 29-35, and also reports that volumes 37-39, Leeward Islands, 1679-1703, contain the correspondence of "governors and other officials in the Leeward islands and Barbados relating to government, trade, piracy, slavery, etc., with draft replies from Blathwayt."

The other item at Colonial Williamsburg (not mentioned in KEI) is the Journal of Nicholas Cresswell, 1774-1777 (MS. 61. 2). This is also available on microfilm (M-1556); it was obtained through interlibrary loan.

While in his early twenties, Nicholas Cresswell left England for the New World. From Liverpool he went directly to Virginia, and a few months later he embarked on a schooner bound for Barbados where he hoped to trade. He arrived at the island on August 31, 1774, after a forty-one day voyage, and stayed until September 17, a period of about three weeks. His journal entries on Barbados (vol. 1, pp. 74-89) briefly record, in a neat and legible hand, observations and comments on a variety of topics: Bridgetown, Holetown, Speightstown, an incident in which he and a companion were stoned by "Negroes," weather, Barbados cotton (which "sells well in Virginia"), a service at the Jewish synagogue, Bridgetown taverns, agricultural exports (sugar, indigo, pimento, cotton), different fruits and vegetables, the milita, planters and their treatment of slaves and keeping of black/colored mistresses, white creole women, black and white funerals; he also regularly names the whites with whom he associated and dined.

Henry E. Huntington Library
San Marino, California

The relatively sizeable collection of Barbados manuscripts at the HL were identified through KEI (pp. 8-26) and the library's catalogs during a visit in August

1980. Below I only describe items that were personally examined or which were not examined (though some were mentioned) by Ingram or were only minimally described in KEI. The user of HL materials, however, should definitely also consult KEI (pp. 8-9, 10-16) for a more complete idea of the HL's Barbados holdings, especially those in the "Ellesmere Papers relating to the British plantations in America and the West Indies, 1608-1700," and the "Blathwayt Papers relating to the British West Indies, 1656/7-1716."

Huntington Miscellany (HM 17). James Hay, 1st Earl of Carlisle, "Papers Relating to Lands in the West Indies Granted to the Merchant Adventurers," 1628-30. Difficult to read, all five documents (nine folio pages) pertain to the earliest settlement of Barbados and the land grants made by Carlisle. These papers, including Carlisle's commission to Charles Wolverston to be governor of Barbados and his well-known 10,000 acre land grant, are seventeenth-century copies of the originals. The five documents have been transcribed and published by Gary Puckrein ("The Carlisle Papers," *JBMHS*, 35, 1978, 300-10), although his interpretation of the documents and their implications for understanding early Barbadian history has been challenged by Peter Campbell (*JBMHS*, 35, 1978, 312-15) and Michael J. Chandler (*JBMHS*, 36, 1979, 72-73); the latter also corrects some minor transcription errors. Photostat copies of these documents are now located in the Barbados Department of Archives.

Stowe Collection (ST 9). James Brydges, "Papers Relating to African Affairs." Includes a thick volume, "Augusta Ann Brydges, her book" (October 1761). One-hundred-and-thirteen pages of this volume are filled with document copies, all of which antedate 1761, including a variety of papers relating to the Royal African Company and the slave trade. The only item specifically treating Barbados (pp. 43-47) is a copy of "Some Remarks on the Trade from Africa to Barbados by Mr. John Ashley, one of the Agents of this said Island" (1725); two other items (pp. 41, 48-52) also relate to the English slave trade to Barbados.

Stowe Collection (ST 28). James Brydges, "A collection of remarkable Papers," ca. 1735. Similar to ST 9 (see above), this forty-two page volume is filled with about forty document copies, two dealing with Barbados. "Letter from Barbados concerning the paper money going to be introduced there Anno 1723" (pp. 1-2); written by "The Barbados Factor," January 1723, the letter notes that paper money was only previously known in Barbados during the administration of Bevil Granville (1703-6). Treating the same issues is "a short view of the present state of Barbadoes as far as relates to the publick debts and the proceedings upon the bill for making paper money," n.d. (pp. 2-4).

Stowe Collection, Grenville Papers (ST G). April 16, 1747-April 2, 1750 (Box 24); April 28, 1750-52 (Box 25). About 130 items, mostly personal and political correspondence. Many letters are originals from Henry Grenville, governor of Barbados (1747-53), to his brother George in London. These letters, reflecting the great affection between the brothers, often deal with family and personal matters, but also treat political and administrative issues in Barbados as well as problems relating to conflicts with the French; included, especially in Box 24, are a variety of papers on the evacuation of St. Lucia, St. Vincent, Dominica, and Tobago. The boxes also contain letters to Grenville from various persons in Barbados, copies of dispatches Grenville sent to the home government, letters to and from the French governor of Martinique, and copies of miscellaneous letters relating to local and international affairs. Although Grenville's letters occasionally comment on nonpolitical conditions and events in Barbados such as epidemics and weather, there is very little information on society and social or cultural life; this collection, however, would be a very useful source on political matters in Barbados during Grenville's administration, his personality and character, and on issues relating to the French wars.

Hispanic Society of America
155th St. and Broadway, New York,
New York

The HSA, which was visited in March 1977 (see also KEI, pp. 196-205), contains only a few items dealing with Barbados. The "Report of the Royal African Company . . . relating to the British Trade with Africa, especially the Slave Trade from

1698 to 1707," 1708/9 (MS. HC 339/8) is "probably a contemporary copy of the original" (KEI, p. 198); it contains abstracts of the number of slaves imported by the company to various islands, the names and numbers of ships, and so forth. This item was published in 1709 as *An Account of the Number of Negroes delivered in to the islands of Barbados, Jamaica, and Antego* (JSH-71).

Another item in the HSA is "Gibraltar, Africa, West Indies, from the Journal of Rev. W. R. Payne, . . . 1822-1825" (MS. HC 378/146). On a number of occasions during 1823 Payne spent brief periods as a chaplain on British naval vessels in the Caribbean. He made several visits to Barbados during this period, but his journal comments (pp. 105-9, 122-23, 152-55, 184-88, 211) are usually brief and confined to limited social subjects. There are a few comments on sexual relations between whites and blacks, especially the propensity of British military and naval officers to take "colored" mistresses and to call them "wives." The longest commentary (pp. 231-44) treats the destruction of the Methodist chapel in 1823, but most pages relating to this event are transcriptions from various printed notices (see, for example, JSH-71).

KEI (items 632, 633) also describes "A Copie Journall of entries made in the Custome House of Barbados," August 10, 1665-April 24, 1667, and a letter from Governor Codrington of Barbados, February 10, 1669; I examined neither of these. Gary Puckrein analyses the former and a related item (see above, Other Bodleian Collections) in *Little England : Plantation Society and Anglo-Barbadian Politics, 1627-1700* (New York: New York University Press, 1984, pp. 57-60).

The Historical Society of Pennsylvania 1300 Locust Street, Philadelphia, Pennsylvania

The Smith Manuscripts (vol. 5, p. 256) contain an anonymously authored and untitled two-page description of Barbados. Dated ca. 1768 in the HSP catalog, where it is also given the title "Account of Barbadoes," this apparently was part of (or intended to be) a longer account for it ends abruptly. This item appears to be part of an account written by John Smith, a Quaker who briefly visited Barbados in 1742. The account has been edited and published by Henry Cadbury (see JSH-71, p. 103), and provides brief comments on weather, fruits and vegetables, the towns, the St. Michael church, Quaker meetings, Carlisle Bay and its forts and shipping, water supplies and local beverages, and the slave population. A relatively large section is devoted to the island's Jewish community and its "large synagogue" where the author observed a service. Other Barbados manuscripts in the HSP are described in JSH-71 (pp. 174-75) and KEI (pp. 257, 258).

John Carter Brown Library Providence, Rhode Island

Various manuscripts in the JCB as of August 1969 are described in JSH-71 (pp. 172-73); the following items were brought to my attention over subsequent years, up to June 1988.

Ms Barb. 17-, Richard Poor, Jr., collection of forty-eight items including letters, notes written from people on the island requesting various types of merchandise, business papers, invoices, lists of goods and merchandise, and fragments of these items dating between 1698 and 1713. All items pertain to business and commercial matters and were written by or to Richard Poor of Bridgetown, a Quaker merchant. Names mentioned include James Bookman, Robert Gibbs, John Lovell, Nathaniel Maverick, John Sandford, Thomas Tryon (see also below, Codex Eng 7). 170-, condensed affidavits regarding personal assault of Antonio Cardona and others upon a "dying soldier." [Barbados, 170-], one page (not examined). 1750-52, about nine detailed invoices for exports of sugar, rum, molasses, and other merchandise shipped from Barbados; shippers include John Maynard, Susanna and Elias Minvielle, Richard Smith and Company. All shipments seem to have been sent to Alexander McKenzie and Co., Norfolk, Virginia (cursorily examined). 1755, original papers in the case of Gibbons vs. Adams with the signatures of Ralph Weekes, president of the Barbados Council, George Taylor, registrar and other officials attached, eight leaves (not examined). 1757, Barbados, articles of agreement (relating to the office of prothonotary of the island, 1757), signed Andrew Stone, Dan Lascelles, G. Maxwell (not examined); letter relating to the office of prothonotary, signed Andrew Stone. May 16, 1757 (not examined), containing "articles of agreement between Andrew Stone and George Maxwell relating to the office of Clerk or Prothonotary," to be held by "James Butcher of Bridgetown" (KEI, pp. 273-74).

Codex Eng. As of January 1975, all the JCB Codex manuscripts were renumbered; thus the ones given in JSH-71 (pp. 172-73) are no longer valid. The following numbers, however, are of the new system. 7, Richard Poor, Jr. "Journall . . . belonging to Richard Poor." Bridgetown, Barbados, 1699-1713. 133 pp. Covers transactions from May 25, 1699 to June 8, 1713. Detailed financial accounts giving the names of customers, sums of money involved, items shipped or sold, etc. Accounts are arranged in chronological order (see also, above). 58, William Parry (manuscript letter book with copies of orders issued by British Vice Admiral William Parry, . . . to Lieut. Henry D'Esterre Darby, from August 10, 1772 to July 23, 1774. Together with Darby's reports to the Admiral.) At head: "His Majesty's ships and vessels employed and to be employed at Barbados the Leeward islands and the seas adjacent" (not examined). 60, John Dovaston, "Agricultura Americana, or Improvements in West-India Husbandry Considered, Wherein the Present System of Husbandry used in England is Applyed to the Cultivation or Growing of Sugar Canes to Advantage . . . wrote in the year 1774." Two manuscript volumes acquired by the JCB in 1968. The preface is dated May 6, 1790. Dovastan, an English lawyer, made his observations on West Indian agriculture during a 1764 trip to Jamaica and another in 1773 to St. Kitts, Nevis, Montserrat, and Jamaica. He intended to publish his volumes, but the American Revolution postponed his plans. A valuable source for the subjects it covers. Written in the form of instructions, or a manual, as to how things should be done rather than an attempt to describe the situation as it is; the latter, however, does come through from time to time. Although focusing on Jamaica, Barbados (which Dovaston did

not visit) is occasionally mentioned, usually in marginal notes, sometimes consisting of direct quotations from Samuel Martin's *Essay on Plantership* (JSH-71); other information on Barbados may be from heresay or published sources. 149, treasurer's account of Barbados, ca. 1755 (not examined). 169, a bound volume, "Trade, West Indies & America." Contains a miscellany of printed and manuscript materials relating to trade issues, including a detailed listing of the monetary value of exports and imports to and from the West Indies and England from Christmas 1739 to Christmas 1773; data are presented on each island, including Barbados (see also KEI, pp. 274-76). 180, Somerset Vale plantation (Journal of the plantation manager, October 13, 1776-June 19, 1778; November 15, 1778-August 10, 1780). Although the JCB catalog had earlier identified Somerset Vale as a Barbados plantation, internal evidence makes it plain that it is a plantation in Jamaica; the JCB catalog entry has since been corrected. The journal provides brief summaries of the weekly and, occasionally, daily main work activities of the slaves, as well as the names and dates of their births and deaths, and occasional notations on weather conditions.

Barbados Map. Surveyed by John Hapcott, October 10, 1646. Acquired by the JCB in June 1982, this very early and unique representation is a surveyed plan of 300 acres of land, the Fort plantation, near Holetown, owned by Captain Thomas Middleton. The late Jeannette D. Black, map curator of the JCB, provides the following descriptive materials in an essay on the map, which also contains a small photographic reproduction of it (Richard B. Arkway Inc., New York, *Catalogue No. XII*, pp. 17-18): "On vellum, in ink and colors, attached to hinged oak boards, drawn in London between 1647 and 1677. . . . 20 1/2" x 24 1/2" . . . . This handsomely colored plan (red, green, turquoise, and gold leaf) . . . . [and] hitherto unknown representation of an area in Barbados as early as 1646 has special historical significance in addition to its suprising beauty." Ms. Black's essay also deals with the surveyor, problems in dating the map, and the cartographic tradition (the Thames School) to which it belongs; this includes a discussion of early political events in Barbados and the land holdings of Thomas Middleton and his son Benjamin. Ms. Black adds in her essay that "there is no way of knowing to what extent the Thames School copyist may have changed or embellished the original drawn by Hapcott in 1646." In any case, the map shows forested areas, an area named "potato peece," and it also contains some small sketches of what was apparently the plantation house and some of its outbuildings; these sketches are small and generalized and are apparently not intended to convey architectural detail. There does not appear to be any cartographic information pertaining to slaves or indentured servants.

Library of Congress
Washington, D.C.

Barbados materials in the LC's Manuscript Division are described in JSH-71 (pp. 175-77) and KEI (pp. 53, 55). Neither of these works, however, mention several letters in the James Madison Papers, written by Henry Lee to Madison in 1813, while the former was in Barbados (see chapter 1, Robert E. Lee, *Memoirs*, 1870). The August 4 and November 17 letters are calendared in *Calendar of the Correspondence of James Madison* (New York, 1894; reprinted 1970, p. 462, while the August 4 letter is published in Robert E. Lee, *Memoirs* (pp. 54-55). A letter from the Manuscript Division's staff (August 14, 1989) states that the LC has no other Henry Lee letters written from Barbados, in either the James Madison Papers or other collections.

In addition, the LC's Division of Geography and Maps holds the private log book of Major A. Kirkham, a British army officer. This bound volume contains brief descriptive passages (and numerous maps) on a variety of geographical areas, including the West Indies from 1798 to 1820. In 1808, Kirkham's ship came into Barbados waters, but did not anchor. The island is very briefly mentioned with respect to military matters, and a superficial geographical description is given; there is also a map of the Atlantic showing the "ship's track" from England to Barbados, through the West Indies, the United States, and then the return to England (pp. 57, 60).

Massachusetts Historical Society
1154 Boylston Street, Boston

The Massachusetts Historical Society's Barbados holdings were briefly noted in JSH-71 (pp. 177-78), primarily on the basis of information provided by the director of the society and Kenneth Ingram in a personal communication before KEI was published. Although KEI does not mention a few of the manuscripts listed in JSH-71, it mentions others and provides greater details on some. The following items are either not mentioned in JSH-71 or mentioned but not described; some of these items were examined subsequent to publication of JSH-71; others have not been personally examined:

Colman Manuscripts. Volume 1, a long letter from Hugh Hall to Benjamin Colman, dated Codrington College, Barbados, March 30, 1720. Hall complains about how Christianity is withheld from "our poor slaves, as if they had no more souls than brutes, & were really a species below us . . . . our clergy seem so ready to slight & ridicule all attempts of their conversion to Christianity even in private families"; and makes a variety of broader comments on the state of religion on the island, including attitudes toward "dissenters" (examined).

Francis Russell Hart Collection. Contains: "a report, dated December 3, 1708 [which] advises the Queen that the petition of Thomas Pinder, merchant of London, for passes for four Spanish ships or others to trade for Negroes between Barbados and New Spain, may not be granted"; a letter from T. Musgrave, W. Erse, E. Bridges, J. Ashe, June 10, 1710, at the Office of Ordnance to the Earl of Sunderland, "enclosing a copy of a letter from Lilly, engineer at Barbados, dated Barbados, December 5, 1709, on the neglected state of the fortifications at Barbados, and asking whether Colonel Lilly should be recalled" (KEI, pp 108, 109).

Hugh Hall Papers. Contain ten letters from Hugh Hall's brother, Richard, in Barbados, "written between July 8, 1733, and September 29, 1737, dealing with business and family matters" (KEI, p. 109). Examined in this collection is Hugh Hall's "Account Book," a small notebook containing the business accounts of this Boston (and Barbados) merchant for the years 1728-33. In a small and cramped hand, the accounts are arranged by year, item, purchaser, etc., and include materials relevant to Thomas Richards and C. Codrington of Barbados; there is also a list of approximately 85 slaves imported from Barbados in 1729, arranged by name of slave and name of purchaser.

Miscellaneous Manuscripts, Bound. Letter from Edward Boylston to Edward Wigglesworth, Professor of Divinity at Harvard, dated Barbados, May 29, 1723; "Concerning the clergy of Barbados—'a melancholy theme'—and the sale of New England fish in Barbados" (KEI, p. 109).

Thomas Prince, "Journal of a Voiage from New England . . . to Berbado's," etc. The journal describes a series of trading voyages from Boston to Barbados, Barbados to London, London to Madeira, Madeira to Barbados, and Barbados to Britain over the period March 29, 1709 to January 30, 1711. The author, who served as ship's chaplain, was first in Barbados from April 22 to September 4, 1709. His brief journal entries, which were not made daily, mainly record the number and kinds of ships and shipping activities in Carlisle Bay, but occasionally take note of other things, such as a small pox epidemic, the 'affecting' spectacle of slavery and its spiritual effects on the island's whites, and some demographic information. There is also a detailed ground plan of St. Ann's fort on the east side of Carlisle Bay. Although Prince again visited Barbados in August, 1710, nothing is said about the island. This item was examined on microfilm at the MHS (PN 110, one reel).

Winthrop Papers. These contain a "group of about 14 letters (1626-73) which relate to Barbados, where Henry Winthrop and, later, Samuel Winthrop settled. They concern tobacco planting, sugar growing and the religious and economic life of the island" (KEI, p. 106). Four of these letters have been published in the Massachusetts Historical Society's *Winthrop Papers*. These include two letters from Henry Winthrop, dated August 22 and October 15, 1627, touching on the island's population groupings, problems of settlement, the need for white servants, problems in tobacco production, and the types and quantities of goods needed for living and farming (vol. 1, pp. 356-57, 361-62)—these are among the earliest known letters written from Barbados. Other letters are from John Winthrop in London to his son Henry, January 30 1628/29, describing the goods he sent Henry, giving advice on commercial issues, and mentioning some family matters (vol. 2, pp. 66-69); and Richard Vines to John Winthrop, Barbados, July 19, 1647, which briefly discusses the problems of tobacco and cotton production and profitability, and notes "next yeare I intend for sugar" (vol. 5, 171-72).

New York Historical Society
170 Central Park West, New York,
New York

KEI lists a relatively large number of Barbados manuscripts, some of which I examined in March, 1977.

Account book of Mathias Lopez, senior, Barbados, 1779-1789. "Includes shop, cash, expenses and sundry accounts of general merchandise"; a microfilm copy is located at UWI (KEI, p. 212).

Letter book and shipping book of Jacobus Van Cortlandt. The letter book of this New York merchant, 1698-1700, "contains copies of letters addressed to merchants and ships' captains in the West Indies, America and England, concerning markets, prices, commodities and slaves"; Barbados is one of the areas from which goods were imported. The shipping book includes printed consignment forms, with handwritten details of goods shipped during 1699-1702, including one consignment to William Sharp in Barbados (see KEI, p. 206, for more details).

Letter book of Theodore Barrell, 1798-1803. "Includes personal, family and business correspondence with persons in London and Barbados. Barrell operated as an attorney and commission agent in Demerara. His principal correspondents in Barbados were William Barton, John Alleyne Beckles, Daniel Broadhead, Mrs. Sarah Gall [Gill?], William Gill, Thomas H. Shepheard, Samuel, John and Thomas Went" (see KEI, p. 215, for more details).

Miscellaneous Manuscripts, Barbados. "Orders, rules and instructions which shall be observed by the Receiver General of Revenue, Barbados," September 12, 1701 (KEI, p. 207).

B. Bancker Papers. Logbook of the sloops *King Solomon* and the *Elizabeth*, kept by John Taylor, master, 1744-47. Includes voyages to Jamaica, Barbados, Anguilla, "with a few pages of accounts of ships' expenditure[s] in Jamaica and Barbados" (KEI, p. 207).

Slavery Collection: Papers relating to slavery and the slave trade in the British West Indies, 1751-1799. According to KEI (p. 207), the West Indian papers "in this large miscellaneous collection . . . consist, in the main, of letters written by ships' captains, agents and merchants in the West Indies to Rhode Island merchants dealing in the slave trade, principally to Samuel and William Vernon, Newport, R.I., and are concerned with the difficulties of the trade, markets and prices in the West Indies, and the health and condition of the slaves." I examined the following Barbados materials mentioned by KEI:

Box 1, Folder B, No. 6. Five very brief letters from Charles Bolton, the Vernons's agent in Barbados. To the Vernons in Rhode Island, February 14, 1755, notifying them that Captain Caleb Godfrey has arrived in Barbados from Africa and is waiting orders on what to do with the slaves he brought; to Captain Godfrey in Rhode Island, March 29, 1755, reporting the sale of "some slaves and the death of two or three," the letter envelope contains a list of the slaves by number and prices paid; to Captain John Brown in Rhode Island, March 29, 1755, pertaining to business matters and slave sales; to the Vernons, March 29, 1755, relating to slave sales; same to same, copy of previous letter, but with a postscript, dated April 14, reporting the death of slave; same to same, May 22, 1755, merely mentioning he heard that Captain Godfrey "came to a good market" in Rhode Island. Folder D, No. 10, letter from Captain Peter Dordin to the Vernons, Barbados, July 17, 1763, notifying them of his arrival at Barbados after a 56-day passage from Africa with 177 slaves, 5 of whom died en route. No. 30, from Captain John Duncan to the Vernons, Barbados, May 21, 1769, reporting his arrival after a passage of 50 days with 76 slaves (10 died en route); slaves are not saleable in Barbados at a good price and he will proceed to Georgia or Virginia. No. 32, same to same, Barbados, March 12, 1771, reporting arrival at Barbados after a 51-day passage with 71 slaves, and "have not lost a slave the whole voyage and [they] are still in very good order and health"; unable to

obtain price of £30 sterling, and will proceed to Virginia after about two weeks in Barbados to repair water caskets, obtain water and provisions, etc. Folder G, Nos. 5, 7, 10, 14, 15, five letters from Caleb Godfrey in Barbados to the Vernons in Rhode Island. January 29, 1755, arrived with cargo of 65 slaves, 4 lost in passage, others are sick; requests permission to stay in Barbados two to three weeks "to recuperate my slaves," then possibly proceed to Jamaica. February 2, 1755, ". . . my slaves was but thin when I arrived owing to a tumbling passage and our decks continually wet for sixteen days. I shall endeavor to get them in good order . . . ." February 4, 1755, fears loss of some of the sick slaves. February 16, 1755, 5 of the sick slaves "is so poor that . . . [they] would not live to South Carolina," and anything they can be sold for in Barbados, "how little," would be "clear gain." February 19, 1755, will sail the next day, his slaves recuperated. Folder H-J, letter from V. Jones in Barbados to the Vernons, May 20, 1769, notifying them of the arrival of two of their slave ships, but he already has on hand 170 slaves he is trying to sell and has advised the captains to go elsewhere with their slaves. Folder K, letter from Samuel and Joseph King, merchants in Barbados, to the Vernons, July 5, 1775, purchased a cargo of 89 slaves which Captain G. D. Sweet has brought from Africa.

Box 2, Folder R, No. 12. Letter from Thomas Rogers in Barbados to the Vernons, September 25, 1765, reporting his arrival from Africa with 57 slaves (9 lost), but they are "very sickly" and is reluctant to proceed to Carolina for fear that most would perish; if he cannot get a suitable price in Barbados, he will proceed to the Leeward islands. Folder S, No. 56, letter from Captain Sweet in Barbados to the Vernons, June 15, 1775, just arrived at Barbados with 61 slaves (5 died in passage), but no market for them and will sail to Dominica.

Box 5. Letter from Valentine Jones in Barbados to Vernons, February 19, 1771, "concerning accounts for brig *Othello* at Antigua and Barbados, 1765 and 1771" (KEI, p. 209).

Box 7. Contains a variety of trading books of slaving vessels. One of the folders (formerly in Box 6), "John Duncan, master, brig *Othello*. Trade Book 1768-69, 1770-71," contains materials relevant to a slaving voyage to Barbados; a daily listing of slaves purchased at Annamaboe, by price, sex and age of each; a "memorandum" itemizing slave deaths (a total of 13) by cause, on the African coast and during the middle passage; and, after arrival at Barbados, a list of disbursements for slaves.

Although KEI (p. 214) mentions the Rufus King Papers, he omits a letter written by Henry Lee to Rufus King, November 19, 1813, while the former lived in Barbados (see chapter 1, Robert E. Lee, *Memoirs*, 1870).

New York Public Library
Fifth Avenue and 42nd Street, New York

NYPL manuscripts relating to Barbados are described in JSH-71 (pp. 179-80), but it is now known that the James Monroe Papers contain several letters from Henry Lee to Secretary of State Monroe, dated Barbados, November 18, 1813 and January 10, 1814; a few others were also written from other Caribbean islands during 1814. The letters treat issues relating to the war between Britain and the United States, and have no materials on Barbados itself (see also chapter 1, Robert E. Lee, *Memoirs*, 1870).

National Archives
Washington, D.C.

Record Group 59 (RG 59). Records of the Department of State, include "consular despatches and related enclosures received by the Department of State from its officers in the British Caribbean area, 1794-1906" (KEI, p. 63). The Barbados records, covering the period 1823-1906 in seventeen volumes, are available on microfilm (T 333). I examined Roll 1 (August 20, 1823-August 4, 1837) in November 1976. The dispatches of the U.S. Consular Commercial Agents (John M. Kankey, Robert Harrison) are usually brief, and their contents are almost entirely concerned with issues of trade between Barbados and the United States.

See KEI (item 192) for reference to United States prisoners in Barbados, 1812-15. In addition, Richard S. Maxwell, in a review of JSH-71, refers to the "records of the Danish Government of the Virgin Islands, 1672-1917, and to the Spanish Governors of Puerto Rico, 1754-1898"; he reports that "both of these foreign language record groups include virtually unused original government documents relating to the Caribbean in general and to many of the islands of the Caribbean specifically, including Barbados" (*The American Archivist*, July-October, 1972, p. 414).

Newberry Library
60 West Walton Place, Chicago, Illinois

A visit to the Newberry in May 1975 and search of its Ayer manuscript collection catalog yielded the following items on Barbados, all of which were examined.

Ayer 276. "An Essay Evenly Discussing the Present Condition and Interest of Barbadoes. And considerations for ye Rendring Peaceable to itselfe and usefull to this common Wealth without the Hazard & ye Charge of sending a ffleet to reduce it." N. D., 20 pp. Deals with the political repercussions of the English Civil War in Barbados and how to win over its inhabitants to the Commonwealth cause; includes brief comments and information on the state of Barbados, for example, population size, produce and exports, and the general value of the island to England, viz., "for this spot is of so much vallue that it may [be] reckoned a jewell, & ye most proud state of ye world may wear it as in a ring. Amongst ye Caribbee islands this disserves to be the Empresse." Although the Ayer catalog provisionally gives this item a 1689 date, this appears to be incorrect: several lines of internal evidence suggest a date of 1650 or 1651, in any case not long before Barbados succumbed to the forces of parliament in early 1652.

Ayer 339. [Plantation Reports], 1717-22. 828 pp. A bound untitled volume (which once belonged to the English statesman Daniel Pulteney) containing reports, letters, instructions to governors, minutes, extracts from miscellaneous documents, etcetera, all of which apparently are copies of originals and are often written in different hands. Pages 1-360 treat the West Indian possessions, many of the items dealing with English claims to St. Vincent, Dominica, and especially St. Lucia; Barbados is regularly mentioned. There are also some materials on the controversy between Governor Lowther and Reverend Gordon in Barbados (see also JSH-71, pp. 22-23).

Ayer 817. "Log of snow *Wennie* on a voyage from Bristol to the West Indies and the North American colonies, from November 1765 to June 1766." 148 pp. The anonymous author sailed with Lord Hope, his ship touching at Barbados on March 3, 1766 after the transatlantic voyage. Staying on the island for about eight days, the author devotes 2 1/2 pages to a description of Barbados, focusing on agriculture, particularly sugar cultivation and manufacturing procedures; there are also some population figures.

Ayer 827. "The State of Barbados." [1684], 28 pp. This is the same as the better-known "An Account of Barbados and the Government Thereof," prepared during the administration of Governor Dutton, located in the British Library (Sloane manuscripts 2441: see JSH-71, p. 135). Various words and phrases in the NL copy have been crossed out in a contemporary hand; the item "is probably an official copy prepared for the Council of Trade and said to have belonged formerly to William Blathwayt" (KEI, p. 77).

Virginia Historical Society
Boulevard and Kensington Avenue,
Richmond, Virginia

Although mentioned in JSH-71 (p. 182) as not having any Barbados materials, KEI (p. 303) records an 1814 letter from Governor Beckwith, and the Lee Family Papers contain some letters that Henry Lee wrote to several members of his family while he was in the West Indies (see chapter 1, Robert E. Lee, *Memoirs*, 1870). The VHS Associate Reference Librarian notified me (personal communication, June 6, 1989) that "the only letter in our collections" written by Henry Lee from Barbados is dated July 7, 1813; it was addressed to his son Henry Lee. However, there may be at least one other letter, September 13, 1813, also addressed to his son Henry (see Royster, *Light-Horse Harry Lee*, 1981, p. 282, note 12).

Yale University: Beinecke Library
New Haven, Connecticut

A visit to the Beinecke in April 1981 and search of its manuscript subject catalog under the heading "Barbados," yielded three items (all on the Osburn shelves, Blathwayt boxes); none were examined. Benjamin Scott, "Account of the customs form for Barbados, 1671-1674"; James Vernon, letter to William Blathwayt, May 14, 1697, giving "news of the Barbados and Virginia convoys and of the Medway fleet"; and another letter from Vernon to Blathwayt, August 1, 1699, "proposing Alexander Skene as secretary of Barbados" and mentioning "Benbow's squadron in the West Indies." These manuscripts do not seem to be mentioned in KEI, which nonetheless includes a variety of other Barbados manuscripts at Yale (KEI, items 44, 45, 46, 48, 51).

Index

WITHDRAWAL